THE
WOMAN'S
WAKEUP

THE
WOMAN'S WAKEUP

How to Shake Up Your Looks, Life, and Love After 50

Lois Joy Johnson

Photography by
MICHAEL WARING

RUNNING PRESS
PHILADELPHIA · LONDON

© 2015 by Lois Joy Johnson
Photography © 2015 by Michael Waring

Published by Running Press,
A Member of the Perseus Books Group

All rights reserved under the Pan-American and
International Copyright Conventions

Printed in China

*This book may not be reproduced in whole or in part, in any form or by
any means, electronic or mechanical, including photocopying, recording,
or by any information storage and retrieval system now known or hereafter
invented, without written permission from the publisher.*

Books published by Running Press are available at special discounts
for bulk purchases in the United States by corporations, institutions, and
other organizations. For more information, please contact the Special
Markets Department at the Perseus Books Group, 2300 Chestnut
Street, Suite 200, Philadelphia, PA 19103, or call (800) 810-4145,
ext. 5000, or e-mail special.markets@perseusbooks.com.

ISBN 978-0-7624-5833-2
Library of Congress Control Number: 2015948602

E-book ISBN 978-0-7624-5834-9

9 8 7 6 5 4 3 2 1
Digit on the right indicates the number of this printing

Designed by Frances J. Soo Ping Chow
Edited by Cindy De La Hoz
Typography: Aire Roman Pro, Aviano Sans, Brandon,
Helvetica Neue, ITC Garamond, and Port Medium

Running Press Book Publishers
2300 Chestnut Street
Philadelphia, PA 19103-4371

Visit us on the web!
www.runningpress.com

For my daughters,

JENNIFER JOLIE AND
ALEXANDRA JADE

CONTENTS

INTRODUCTION

THIS BOOK IS YOUR GPS TO THE NEW BOOMERINA AGE, WHERE WOMEN 50+ WEAR SKINNY LEATHER JEANS, SLEEVELESS DRESSES, CAGED BOOTIES, DATE ONLINE, GET BOTOX, AND TAKE SPIN CLASSES.

We *know* we're smart, sassy, evolved, experienced, adventurous, and sexy but we have tweaked, even that last virtue, to fit our new mind-set, roles, and lifestyles. Sexy after 50 doesn't mean wearing heels and minis (though some of us do!). It means being a risk taker, relishing your independent spirit and energetic attitude. It means keeping the glint in your eye, that spark of mischief, and not being a pushover for people who say no. It means betting on your plucky instincts and guts to get your foot in the door, enhance your social life, and find new ways to flaunt your brains and beauty. We Boomer Babes or B-Babes (as I've renamed us) are street-smart, saucy, stylish, seasoned, and ready to go.

Becoming a B-Babe has status. It's like being invited to flash a black Amex Centurion instead of the standard green card. Of course, we still rant about menopause aftershock . . . hot flashes, dry skin, wrinkles, brown spots, thinning hair, and hormonal weight gain come with the privilege of age, too. Nothing inspires us more than our peers—women who continue to redefine age. In this book you'll meet an inspiring group of diverse, enthusiastic, forward-thinking women who question and defy every stereotype of what it means to be older. Photographed by the amazing Michael Waring in their own wardrobe favorites, each woman goes way beyond trends to reflect her own very personal style and opinions.

You'll find as you read this book that being a brilliant, sensual, irresistible woman over 50 is not a one-size-fits-all trip. *The Woman's Wakeup* is your navigation tool and marks the best routes and side roads, U-turns, and shortcuts. As expert life jugglers, our balancing act now has new elements and *those* keep changing and evolving, including our looks, friendships, work, and even our love life. Use the inspirational info in these pages and the charismatic ambassadors I'll introduce you to as an opportunity to change direction, find your way, and fearlessly update your life.

I'm one of you! Yes, I happen to be an award-winning journalist and beauty/fashion/lifestyle expert known for my experience and significant contributions to changing sociological attitudes toward age, but I'm down there in the trenches with you. My work is focused on celebrating all women 50+, solving their beauty and style issues and concerns about age. As beauty and fashion director of *MORE* magazine for over a decade, I helped make age not only acceptable but also appealing. Frankly, no other beauty and fashion writer/editor/blogger/ columnist has my hands-on experience with you, my B-Babe girlfriends. I've been through a lot of the same experiences and mistakes and write a lot about them in my weekly AARP.org column. I'm married for the third (and final!) time, have 2 fabulous adult daughters (Jennifer and Alexandra), 3 adult stepchildren (Allison, Paula, and David), 2 amazing grandsons (Ian and Ryan), and am part of an extended family of 5 grandmas. I've had to adapt. Yet I've learned to balance my life—husband, work, friends, interests, and a personal to-do list that never ends.

• • • • •

USE THIS BOOK 3 WAYS:

1 IF YOU WANT TO PUSH THE RESET BUTTON AND START OVER.

Nothing like a few speed bumps to initiate change. Divorce, friendships gone toxic, job loss, and financial upsets will do it. So do weight gain and hormonal shifts, hair loss, and sun damage showing up head to toe. The tricks I've learned as a beauty and fashion editor and a woman 50+ with a "been there, done that" track record will reboot you fast. Learn how to look amazing on social media, fatten up your thinning hair, and decide on the best body spots for a celebratory tattoo or 2.

2 IF YOU'RE TOTALLY STUCK IN AN AGE RUT AND WANT FRESH HOW-TO ADVICE.

The looking good bar has been raised thanks to familiar media faces like Christie Brinkley, Ellen DeGeneres, Helen Mirren, Hoda Kotb, Kathie Lee Gifford, Kris Jenner, and Viola Davis. They keep tweaking their style and look all the time. We *know* they deal with the same beauty and style issues we do. Find out how to make hearing aids chic, get permanent makeup, wear fake hairpieces with panache, deal with saggy boobs, grow out gray hair fast, give up wearing heels *or* start wearing them again, which glasses are your best bet, and avoid bad cosmetic surgery and get it right.

3 IF YOU'RE ADJUSTING TO NEW SITUATIONS AND PEOPLE.

We are an alien species, born before technology, rap music, and takeout, but we're also super-fast adapters who keep changing with the times—we want to stay contemporary, current, and informed. I'll tell you how to travel solo and love it, get past HR in your job hunt, drop the fear of your high school reunion, and get your derriere off the sofa and back into a social life.

Act like you're an 11 in a world of 10s . . . because you're about to become one.

MEET MY FRIENDS

THROUGHOUT THESE PAGES YOU'LL GET TO KNOW
11 OTHER WOMEN WHO'VE COME THROUGH
THEIR OWN "WAKEUP/SHAKEUP" TRANSITIONS WITH
GUTS, GRACE, AND GUSTO.

ALISON HOUTTE

Ex-model, vintage fashion pro, crack tennis player, online dating whiz, daring dresser, leopard-print addict, and owner of Hooti Couture in Brooklyn, New York.

AUDREY SMALTZ

Founder and CEO of the Ground Crew, the A-list management team for top NYC designer runway shows. Charismatic keynote speaker, philanthropist, wife, grand-mother, and "woman of a certain hip age."

BRENDA COFFEE

Founder and CEO of 1010 Park Place, an online content and retail site for women 40+. Breast cancer survivor and creator of the Breast Cancer Sisterhood, an online resource for women with breast cancer and their families. Adventure junkie and risk taker who lives with one foot in NYC and the other in Texas.

CAROL E. CAMPBELL

Group Strategic Director at Hearst Media, nicknamed "the Moneymaker," Bikram yoga and horseback riding devotee, dog lover, dating expert and provocateur, gourmet "foodie," and shopping fanatic.

DONNA BUNTE

Model and founder of Donna Bunte Whole Health in Greenwich, Connecticut. Chinese medicine doctor and nutritional advisor, healthy-eating advocate, married mom of 2 college kids, fabulous cook, and global traveler.

JEANNINE SHAO COLLINS

Publisher of *MORE* magazine (for the second time!), energetic dealmaker and networker, guaranteed solution-finder, luxury lover, dress fan, and lipstick collector. Married mom of 3.

KAREN OLIVER

Founder and CEO of Karen Oliver and Associates, an NYC public relations agency. Fierce advocate for luxury French beauty brands, couture-quality seamstress who makes lots of her gorgeous wardrobe, lover of one-of-a-kind items from Antigua to Marrakesh.

MAURY ROGOFF

Founder and CEO of Maury Rogoff PR & Marketing, NYC and Palm Beach. Mom of 2 twentysomething kids, card-and-letter sender. Famous for her streaky blonde mane and ability to go from sweats to black-tie-ready in 5 minutes.

MYRNA BLYTH

VP and Editorial Director of AARP, founding editor of *MORE* magazine, publishing-industry legend who hobnobs with celebs. Adores eye make-up, dresses, and heels. Global traveler, Glam-ma of 2.

NANCY GANZ STEIR

Creator of Bodyslimmers by Nancy Ganz and FashionFantasyGame.com. Entrepreneur who invented the modern shapewear business back in the '80s. Married mom of 2 who balances spinning, treadmill, and daily doses of 85 percent dark chocolate. Had a prophylactic double mastectomy and reconstruction and swapped bras for tanks!

RENE SYLER

Founder of her own Good Enough Mother Media brand, author, and cohost of the *Exhale* talk show. Prefers comfort and sports clothes to designer duds, loves her wild curly hair and show-offy triceps. Big on weight training and eating high protein. Married mom of 2.

CHAPTER ONE:

LIFE IN TRANSITION

STAY FOXY, SEASONED, AND WISE.

That's what *The Woman's Wakeup* is—a map to keep you steady and on track during this big adventure into the rest of your life.

Ask any woman 50+ how her life is going. She's likely to smile like an Indianapolis 500 winner and say, "I'm in transition." We're all on that track now and the race has become a journey with plenty of unexpected exit ramps and turns. Fortunately, we're in the driver's seat and not averse to switching lanes, downshifting, putting the pedal to the metal, or taking a back road to get where we want. From the minute we cross the half-century line, we're marked women. The media chases us with come-ons for surviving the *next* 50: "How to live abroad for less than your gym membership!" "Cosmetic surgery cruises for seniors!" "10 foods that prevent menopause madness!" "The secret de-ager of the decade (no *really* this time we mean it)!" It's enough to knock us—a generation of opinionated, feisty, spirited, mature women—off our Manolos and into a pair of Birkenstocks (and not the fur-lined ones, either). Well, *of course* we want to look better than ever (why wouldn't we?), but

BRENDA COFFEE

Reinvention and transition should be line items on my résumé. My life has been one adventure after the other. I searched for minerals and crystals in abandoned silver mines; dove for Spanish relics in the Caribbean; dug for Mayan artifacts. In between adventures, I've started and run companies. It took me a long time to pull myself together after my third husband, James, died. When Yahoo asked me to speak to an invitation-only audience of Fortune 100 companies at Internet Week in NYC on marketing to women over 45, I had an ah-ha moment and wrote the business plan for 1010 Park Place, a content and shopping site for older women and the basis of my future.

keeping our brains and bodies active and our attitude up is part of the plan, too. So we need answers we can trust.

That's what *The Woman's Wakeup* is—a map to keep you steady and on track during this big adventure into the rest of your life.

So far so good. We seem to have made it to 50 and LOL to all those cynics (young and old) who said we'd never adapt to technology. Well, we're bragging, boasting, and broadcasting just like Millennials do. We tweet crossing the finish line of our first marathon at 52, Instagram photos of our "healthy" kale and egg white omelet and our adorable rescue dog saved from a shelter last weekend, and, of course, we Pinterest our shoe and bag obsessions for all. Everything we do, say, think, and feel is now a news-breaking report. Aging inconspicuously? Not exactly. Not us!

AGE IS APPROPRIATE AND AWESOME

After years of brainwashing our mantra truly is "live in the moment." We do try. Taking classes (at a local college or trade school), launching a new career (even an entry-level job but WTH!), or starting our own business (from a boutique to a home organization service) is the new normal for women our age. Those of us now single venture into the "new" dating scene (this time online!) and reconnect with old

> And yet, the most priceless thing about us is this: **we are women with a past.**

RENE SYLER

One of the things I love about this new chapter in my life is that at 52 I'm old enough to be wise but young enough to have fun. The life you plan is not the life you lead. My blueprint for success was to get a college degree, work hard 30 years, have a family, then retire comfortably. The reality was I worked hard to get to the pinnacle of my career as a national cohost of CBS's *The Early Show*, only to have the bottom drop out. In 2 years I lost my job and I lost my breasts (in a preventative bilateral mastectomy). So here's my advice to women who fear change: You won't grow while you're comfortable or be comfortable while you're growing. Some women, like me, are natural thrill-seekers; if we're not flying by the seat of our pants, we're not living. There are no shortcuts, just do the work. Not everyone will like you. Let that be their problem. Be the architect of your own life, not the carpenter of someone else's.

"friends" on Facebook to expand our social world. We attempt scary things (because whatever we are, we're not wimps!) like surfing, scuba diving, rock climbing, or even sex again . . . maybe even with a young, hip guy!

And yet, the most priceless thing about us is this: we are women with a past. Our stash of wisdom, wit, knowledge, survival skills, experience, and the ability to connect with people face-to-face (a vanishing art), are our treasured assets.

Of course, after 6 or 7 decades of living we have a hefty cache of opinions, a built-in capacity to edit truth from BS and say so, and the ability to have a great day totally without any electronic gadgets. In other words, we are senior-level gurus who are still works in progress—and that's the way we like it.

LET'S DISH

Your life is a lot like that of every other woman your age. Don't be surprised. Regardless of individual finances, health, relationships, work situations, or where you call home, we *all* stress out, wonder what to do, and laugh over the same stuff. I'm certainly no therapist, but as a longtime beauty-fashion expert, I've worked with thousands of women over 50—famous and not—who've shared their thoughts and feelings with me over a pair of Spanx and a rack of clothes. Nothing bonds women together like a fitting room! We're all in this together, rethinking the rest of our lives.

DONNA BUNTE

I've been in transition for years with one foot in modeling and the other in Chinese medicine. After some health issues, I began studying nutrition, cooking, homeopathy, herbal medicine, Ayurveda, Chinese medicine, and meditation yoga and that became my focus. Chinese medicine impressed me as a complete system of theory, herbal medicine, dietary therapy, acupuncture, acupressure, meditation, exercise, and an overall lifestyle. I started my Donna Bunte Whole Health practice 20 years ago in NYC while continuing to model. Then when my husband and I moved to Connecticut, I established my office there. My latest endeavor is studying to become a certified integrative nutrition coach, which I am *really* enjoying. With 2 kids in college, I'm excited about the next phase of my life!

YOU'RE FAR FROM ALONE.
LET ME ASSURE YOU WE ALL:

ACT ON IMPULSE.

It's okay to jump in, take a chance, try something new, and shake things up. Some decisions seem spontaneous, but the ideas have been lurking. For example, you wave a magazine photo of Robin Wright's short cut in front of your stylist and say "Okay, chop it all off" during your usual blowout. It feels spur-of-the-moment but probably has been simmering since last season's *House of Cards*. Or you're at the dermatologist for a checkup and decide to Botox *now*! Being impromptu is a healthy part of transition and keeps life lively.

BUT GET TOTALLY STRATEGIC, TOO.

We can be logical and realistic. We have to be. Every woman I know is worried about staying economically stable now that living way into our 80s, 90s, and even beyond seems possible. Our work lives go on and on, like it or not. We do our "money" homework about everything. None of us wants to be frivolous so we check out the best for less online—from fashion to restaurants, vacations to blow-dry salons, comparing prices and hunting down deals like truffle-sniffing dogs. When it comes to thinking about the future, planning keeps our stress levels manageable.

ARE WILLING TO MAKE CHANGES.

Flexibility is one of our best characteristics. Of course, we've spent years aspiring to the best of everything but now who needs it all? Downsizing from a townhouse to a condo, a suburban sprawl to an urban studio loft, a Mercedes to a Honda, designer labels to J. Crew feels smart and adventurous. We like the opportunity to edit, change, and remake ourselves and our lives. Relocation to another town or state? Maybe, when perks like gorgeous scenery or weather, more things to do, available work for seniors, and a more affordable lifestyle are part of the deal. Even moving back to our hometown and family-run business sounds good. And why stay in a stale, unhappy relationship? Spirited women 50+ are divorcing longtime husbands and moving on, dating and finding new lifestyles and friends. Sell our vintage Donna Karan and Armani on eBay or a consignment site? Great idea! We just might pick up some cash, pay off that Visa bill—and feel guilt-free about letting it all go.

PURSUE OLD DREAMS.

How about old passions that got left behind? With mysterious timing they return to our brains like homing pigeons. Maybe your personal love of baking, yoga, dogs, painting furniture, clothes, or gardening could stir up a new work opportunity. Why not sell your gourmet cupcakes at a local farmer's market or your spectacular raisin walnut bread to local bakeries? Why not start a furniture restoration business at home, work at a local boutique, start a neighborhood dog-walking/pet-sitting service, teach yoga at a health club, or a gardening class for seniors at the community center? If not now…when?

LET PERSONAL HISTORY GUIDE US.

For better or worse the past reminds us what *not* to do this time around and points the way to options! How disastrous was trying to learn Spanish from language tapes? At 50 a Beginners Spanish adult-ed class at the high school would probably get you on the road to everyday fluency fast in a more relaxed social setting. How about all the job interviews where our prep wasn't up to speed? Now we do serious homework, lock-in our spiel, and dress like C-suite execs.

····

Q: We're all anxious about change. So what's your reason?

A: Making a big mistake. Running out of time, money, ideas, and options.

You don't have to go to extremes. Small changes are fine and provide incentive for bigger ones. Even celebs and top business executives are not exempt from exploring changes, small and huge. Remember when Michelle Obama, at almost 50, cut bangs (and then grew them out!) or when Helen Mirren at 67 dyed her grayish locks punk pink for a red carpet night (then went back to blonde and nailed a big cosmetic contract)? How about when Katie Couric became the first female solo anchor of TV evening news at 50, left that for her own talk show, and then moved on at 57 to be Global News Anchor at Yahoo. Spinning her talent in new ways led to new gigs. We all have the itch to move on and take risks. Let's not forget folk-art heroine Grandma Moses, either. She didn't start cranking out paintings till well into her 70s! We're all betting on a gutsy future.

····

BEEN THERE,
DONE THAT

At 40 I had no idea what my life at 50 would be. Although I adored my job as beauty and fashion director at *MORE* magazine, 11 years into that groove a little transition flipped me from NYC full-time editor to a freelance lifestyle. Suddenly I was writing beauty and style books and online columns for women 50+. I moved to my husband's apartment, leaving behind a cache of designer clothes and gained a clientele of major beauty and fashion brands, celebs (I "ghostwrite" their books!), and private clients seeking makeover guidance as they shift gears. Do I miss my old magazine job, life, or home? Nope! I concentrate on what's possible rather than impossible and I never look back.

LOIS'S TUTORIAL OF TRICKS #1

WE GET IT! 10 TRUTHS TO LIVE BY NOW

The media sure does a great job of whipping up trends and breaking news into a complex drama of what we must do, must have, and never do again. One minute they say one thing and contradict it a week later. These reversals make us queasy. Some alerts and "rumors" are actually based on truth while others are pure bunk. These 10 are the ones to remember.

1 SLEEP HELPS YOU DODGE WRINKLES, BROWN SPOTS, WEIGHT, AND STRESS.

Really, girlfriends, solve the insomnia issue because sleep is essential! If you snooze you lose, and I mean everything from aging skin to extra pounds. Three super NYC dermatologists agree, so curl up in bed and read on.

Dermatologist Dr. Doris Day, who is "one of us" and has a celebrity-packed practice, says, "Hormonal changes can make sleep difficult during and after menopause. First try a stress-reducing holistic approach. Listening to relaxation tapes with a soothing, positive message works for me. Ask your doctor about a very low dose of antidepressant—not a medical dose for true depression—just enough for a knockout when sleep really seems impossible."

Dr. Debra Jaliman, with a clientele of top models, editors, and media stars, who also teaches at the Mount Sinai School of Medicine, says, "During

NANCY GANZ STEIR

Not only am I wiser now, but I know myself better and my strengths and weaknesses. I'm an entrepreneur, a doer, a problem solver, a creator, and a visionary. I enjoy the start-up action of an idea and feel more alive than ever when I'm involved in one. I love learning about health, neurophysiology, and psychology. I feel ageless when I'm learning new things and creating, old when I'm not.

sleep, skin cells repair and rejuvenate, your body temperature drops, and hormonal changes push blood flow to the skin, so serious night treatments like retinol helps to boost collagen and speed up cell turnover." Two that get rave reviews are RoC Retinol Correxion Deep Wrinkle Serum and RoC Retinol Correxion Eye Cream.

Dr. Joshua Zeichner, Director of Cosmetic and Clinical Research in Dermatology at Mount Sinai Hospital, adds, "your skin works on natural circadian rhythms so disrupting your sleep cycle

➤ **Soak in a fragrant tub before snoozing.** Aromatherapy—a method of using certain scents to improve mood—can't *cure* insomnia but bathing in lavender or vanilla-based bath salts, oils, or bubbles before bed can relax and calm. These aromatherapy scents have a subtle anxiety-reducing effect and are easy to find at drug and health-food stores. I love those by Dr. Teal's, Ahava, and Kneipp.

Sleep deprivation can also cause weight gain!

interferes with healing, leading to more fine lines, wrinkles, and crepey skin later on." If that doesn't convince you to hit the sack, how about this zinger: lack of quality sleep might be why your clothes don't fit!

"Sleep deprivation can also cause weight gain!" says Dr. Jaliman. "It lowers the appetite-suppressing hormone leptin and ramps up the hunger-encouraging one—ghrelin."

Perfect. So we insomniacs reach for carbs—sweet, salty, fatty snacks during nightly kitchen raids and end up complaining our new jeans (ordered online at 3:00 a.m.) won't zip. You need to:

➤ **Power down your computer, cell, and TV early in the evening.** Stop caffeine intake hours before bed. A glass of wine may cause drowsiness, but your sleep will be disrupted. And if you stay up late to work, your stress hormone cortisol goes up, too, so expect to be cranky, nervous, and hyper the next day.

➤ **Splurge on a silk pillowcase and aim for 7 to 9 hours of Zzz's.** Switching to a silk pillowcase is a legendary de-aging fix with merit. Dr. Jaliman says, "a silk case has more 'slip' than cotton so it minimizes compression." And less friction equals less damage and breakage for dry, thin, processed hair, too!

➤ **Note how you sleep.** The American Academy of Dermatology has reported that sleeping in certain positions night after night increases permanent facial lines. Sleeping on your tummy with your face mushed into the pillow can etch brow creases and expression grooves. Even sleeping on your side presses wrinkles into your cheeks, chest, and chin. If you favor one side, you'll see more lines, deeper wrinkles, and sagging skin on that half. Check your mirror profiles!

2 A TATTOO AT 50 IS OKAY BUT KNOW WHICH ONE, WHERE, AND WHY.

Getting a tattoo should be a deliberate, thought-out move, not an impulsive one. The reasons I hear most are: "to bond with my daughter (she has a heart on her ankle, too)," "to remind and inspire me," "to celebrate a major zero birthday," "to feel youthful," and to "honor a clean bill of health." Other women just want to imprint what matters to them now—a religious symbol, a date, initials, or an astrological sign. Getting a tattoo at 50+ flouts tradition. You've probably thought about it . . . maybe a tiny, discreet one. Tattoos are permanent so let's be clever about where to put one, its size, and complexity.

The big question is: how's it going to look on skin that may sag, bloat, spread, get brown spots, or wrinkle with age and weight fluctuations? Skip your arms, back, legs, thighs, tummy, and derriere. A slim, bony spot like your wrists, ankles, or tops of your feet are better choices.

➤ **Opt for graceful and small.** A delicate vine or bow tie ribbon bracelet tattoo at the wrist, or a sprinkle of tiny stars peeping above your ankle booties, can be elegant and subtly avant-garde. Don't tat anything you may regret—menacing Goth skulls or daggers, big clichés on your lower back (known as a "tramp stamp"), or hearts with your love's initials since the relationship may not last but the ink will. Getting a tattoo is not pain-free—it feels like sticking sunburn with a pin and takes hours to do. Hours of pure discomfort.

➤ **Make sure your tattoo artist is an authorized pro.** Hopefully he or she is a licensed or registered artist recognized by the board of health. You want to avoid infection or Hepatitis C! He'd better have a good eye, too—with an emphasis on skill and aesthetics. Ask to see his/her work or get references from friends who have tats you admire. You want Michelangelo, not a cartoonist.

➤ **Expect an ugly phase at first.** Sun exposure, self-tanning, and sweat aggravate a fresh tattoo so get one in cool weather or winter. Expect an uncomfortable, unappealing phase before it settles. For those wavering or with sensitive skin, Dr. Zeichner suggests "sticking to a single color tattoo in black since red hues are associated with a higher allergic risk. Vibrant colors are more difficult to laser away if you change your mind." And FYI, laser removal is not exactly a walk in the park, either—it's nasty, costly, and time-consuming.

➤ **Put health and skin safety first.** Dr. Jaliman says, "Make sure the shop has a medical grade autoclave to sterilize equipment and the artist uses a new sterile needle and wears sterile gloves. Remove the bandage within 3 to 6 hours of getting fresh ink, gently wash the area, pat dry, and apply a very thin layer of antibiotic ointment or Aquaphor. Repeat twice a day. If there is any pain, redness, swelling, or oozing, see your dermatologist immediately." And avoid covering moles with a tattoo. It interferes with your ability to see changes and check for skin cancer.

THE BIG QUESTION IS: how's it going to look on skin that may sag, bloat, spread, get brown spots, or wrinkle with age and weight fluctuations? Skip your arms, back, legs, thighs, tummy, and derriere. Slim, bony spots like your wrists, ankles, or tops of your feet are better choices.

3 GROWING OUT YOUR HAIR TO GRAY IS SO NOT A BIG DEAL ANYMORE.

What are you waiting for? You've been gazing at Jamie Lee Curtis, Emmylou Harris, Glenn Close and wondering haven't you? Gray hair is officially cool, though it's not for everyone. We approach going for gray with the same mind-bending mix of fear and anticipation as a divorce or a face-lift. Here's how to do it with tips from color genie Julius Michael of the Julius Michael Salon in Scarsdale, New York:

➤ **Skip retouching your base color.** The toughest part is the initial first 2 inches of the grow-out phase, when you shouldn't touch your color. Yeah, you might look a little root-y and unkempt, but adding volume and tousling your hair will help disguise a solid line where gray and processed color meet. And you can use a wash-out root touch-up powder like Color Wow for days when you need some polishing.

See what color gray comes in. Your gray may be a salt-and-pepper mix, stripe-y, or one solid hue. You can never be absolutely sure.

➤ **Add highlights or a mix of highlights and lowlights.** A salon colorist can easily do this to mesh incoming grays with your chemical color—but again, no touching the base color at all. This strategy adds silvery glints at the roots so you don't have an obvious ring of white or ash.

To keep gray that's flat, muddy, drab, or mousey flattering, continue to throw in a few highlights twice a year. You'll still be gray but your best gray.

Superstar colorist Brad Johns, of the Brad Johns Color Studio at the Samuel Shriqui Salon in NYC, adds, "Silvery highlights will add texture and dimension to thin gray hair for a thicker look. White, platinum, silvery gray usually works best when skin has warm golden undertones, a rich healthy color." Go a shade warmer in face makeup or just add a golden shimmery bronzer to compensate for the cool influence of gray.

Julius Michael adds "Silvery highlights will add texture and build up thin gray hair for a thicker look. Add a clear gloss treatment to restore luster."

4 EAT HEALTHIER TO IMPROVE THINNING HAIR… NOT JUST YOUR SHAPE.

By 50 most women complain about skimpy, thinning hair. Two reasons: the growth, resting, and shedding cycle has slowed and our hair is showing damage from years of poor nutrition, heat-styling, and chemical processing. Thin hair usually hits just as weak nails, saggy skin, and extra pounds do, too. Eat for your hair's sake and you'll improve the rest. NYC hair specialist and restoration surgeon Dr. Robert Dorin says, "Extreme diets deplete your body of nutrients. Women 50+ need high-quality calories, especially protein, omega-3, vitamins, and minerals. Focusing on 'weight' as justification for a very strict diet may be damaging all the cells of your body, not only your hair." A few more tips from the doctor:

➤ **If you're a vegetarian be sure to get sufficient protein and omega-3.** "Hair is 97 percent protein, so eating eggs, Greek yogurt, chicken, beef, fish, lentils, and veggies like broccoli and kale can help regrow hairs shed during the resting phase. Vegans need to step up their intake of legumes like green peas and chickpeas, grains like quinoa, nuts and nut butters, beans, tofu, edamame, chia seeds, and nondairy milk (like almond or rice milk)."

➤ **Specific foods help condition dry hair and scalp, for a healthy look.** "Add vitamin-A foods like pumpkin seeds, apricots, carrots, mangoes, sweet potatoes, and cantaloupe, as well as omega-3 foods like salmon, sardines, walnuts, and avocado" to your weekly rotation.

MYRNA BLYTH

Many women at 50+ who say they are "in transition" have left a job that defined them. As our lives changed, women did, too, and the emphasis became more on ourselves and our achievements—even those who had families. AARP Life Reimagined is about the extra 30 or 40 years of life women now have. We're a diverse group in many ways. I remember doing focus groups with women when we were starting *MORE* magazine. One group said they wanted to watch *Oprah*, the second group wanted to be a guest on *Oprah*, and the third wanted to *be* Oprah!

5 ADMIT YOU CAN'T HEAR AND *DO SOMETHING* ABOUT IT!

Get over the vanity issue already. Hearing aids, or as I refer to them, "listeners,"changed my life. After years of saying "What?!" and bluffing my way through conversations on the phone (where I couldn't read lips), at parties, and noisy restaurants, I got my ears medically checked by an ear, nose, and throat specialist. Then an audiologist analyzed what kind of device suited my hearing loss, which

➤ **If your "listeners" are the visible behind-the-ear types** like mine (They're from Widex, FYI), make them and your glasses a stylish team. This is super important if you wear your hair short, often tuck it behind your ears, or pull it back in a ponytail. Choose a contemporary subtle metallic or a trendy neon shade for the listeners and black, tortoise semi-rimless or rimless glasses.

Hearing aids are now miniature earbud-looking devices.... And they're hi-tech sexy!

was hereditary and extensive. It explained why I paused and replayed every episode of *Homeland* and *Downton Abbey* and cranked up the Sirius radio in the car. For me, hearing aids were these enormous flesh-toned plugs that looked like Mr. Potato Head noses. Well, guess what?

Hearing aids are now miniature earbud-looking devices that are digital and use computer technology. And they're hi-tech sexy!

Buy the best ones for your degree of loss, ear physicality, dexterity, aesthetics, and finances. Due to a malformation of my ear canal, my listeners are not totally internal, but they are chic as hell. A slim blond-toned "device" goes behind my ear and connects via a clear wire to a tiny transparent receiver in my ear canal. I hear *everything* and control noise level, too.

➤ **If your hearing aids are invisible and go inside your ears there's no conflict.** Choose frames as conservative or statement-making as you like.

➤ **For an extra confidence lift in social situations or at work** (ageism is a factor), keep your hair at least chin length for coverage and boost volume at the sides with subtle layers.

➤ **Get a hearing-help phone.** Switch your home phones to cordless handsets that stream sound directly to your hearing aids to clarify and amplify conversations. They improve sound even when I'm not wearing my hearing aids. For those in your family with "normal" hearing they just function as regular phones.

6 BUY GIVE-BACK BEAUTY AND STYLE BRANDS. FEELS SOOO GOOD!

I don't drive a hybrid, have a compost heap, veggie garden, or solar panels, though I do recycle, buy organic food, worry about climate change, polar bears, whales, bushfires in California, cyclones, tsunamis, tornados, flooding, and carbon pollution. Buying and wearing socially responsible brands with a heart can lift your spirits every day.

▶ **Go somewhat green-ish.** No need to jump on the entire organic green bandwagon or totally reject chemicals, either. "Natural" and "hi-tech" beauty products are both often a combo of natural and chemical and who's to say that's so bad? Simple plant ingredients and botanical oils can improve mature skin and hair. Be willing to compromise—some products do include preservatives and chemicals to make all those organics work at an optimum level. Buy with your head, heart, and ultimately what works to make you look and feel great.

▶ **Some beauty brands have earned our respect with a reputation for their philanthropic efforts.** They believe in supporting health and social issues with a consistent message, funding, campaigns, and efforts that reach far beyond looking good—and it's not just for show. L'Oréal Paris founded the Women of Worth Program, which honors and awards women who are making a difference in their communities. The Laura Mercier beauty brand started the Laura Mercier Ovarian Cancer Fund to raise awareness and research to diagnose, treat, and support women with this disease. The Estée Lauder Company's Breast Cancer Awareness Campaign has raised more than $58 million for research, while Kiehl's Since 1851 supports amfAR, the Foundation for AIDS Research. Davines haircare is produced using energy from renewable resources with zero-impact packaging and reduced use of plastic to stay committed to safe-guarding the planet's biodiversity.

▶ **Fashion brands have a heart, too.** Warby Parker, the online glasses site, has a "Buy a Pair, Give a Pair" program (you buy new frames, another pair is donated), Toms footwear provides a week of clean water or a pair of shoes for every pair sold, and Eileen Fisher supports Fair Trade, human rights, and leadership programs for women and women-owned businesses.

7 AN ANNUAL EYE EXAM AND UPDATED FRAMES ARE A MUST.

Age-related eye changes are normal after 50 but require a checkup, same as your gyno. New frames offer the fastest style fix possible, too!

➤ **A comprehensive eye exam can reveal problems.** Don't just rely on your old Rx to fill new frames. If you're experiencing serious vision changes or eyestrain at any time, get checked at your optometrist or ophthalmologist for glaucoma, cataracts, or macular degeneration. All are serious health issues.

➤ **Buy ready-made readers in a strength right for you.** If you don't wear prescription lenses for close-up vision, fashionable readers in a magnification strength right for you make scanning menus, newspapers, magazines, books, your Kindle, or iPad easier and sexier to peer over. Try leopard or turquoise! Check eyebobs.com for chic choices.

➤ **Get your sunglasses updated, too.** Whether sun-readers or prescription lenses, be sure they're UV-protected and dark enough to do the job if you're driving. Dark green, gray, or brown cut glare on the road and reduce eyestrain without color distortion. Light blue and violet lenses are good for foggy, misty, snowy, hazy days when you're just taking a walk or running errands. Rosy pink lenses are comforting to sensitive eyes and help reduce eyestrain.

8 YEARLY MOLE AND FULL-BODY SKIN CANCER CHECKS ARE NOT NEGOTIABLE!

You can't wait, stall, or play guessing games with basal or squamous cell skin cancer and melanoma. Checking your moles and other doodads against an online chart is not acceptable or smart. Any skin growth or mole that changes in color, size, texture, or continues to itch, crust, scab, or bleed, needs a skilled dermatologist's observation. For women who fear scarring from too many biopsies, new technologies and tools can decrease the need for multiple procedures.

Find a dermatologist who uses MelaFind, a diagnostic device that identifies specific moles requiring biopsies. Unlike the human eye it views way beneath the skin for a three-dimensional view.

Dermatologist Dr. Doris Day says, "Mela-Find uses multispectral light technology to analyze and separate unusual noncancerous moles from potentially deadly ones in a non-invasive way—it eliminates unnecessary cutting. All info is stored electronically for future tracking and you get a printout of the diagnosis and visual imaging in case you change doctors or move."

9 YOU CAN MAKE YOUR GOOD SHOES AND BAGS LAST FOREVER.

We love nothing better than shoes and bags and online shopping only fuels our addiction. No need to preserve your accessories like they're going into the Metropolitan Museum of Art, but make an effort! My ancient black Chanel 2.55 bag circa 1984 looks fresh out of the box thanks to babylike swaddling in a flannel bag and tender touch-ups. It's all pretty simple.

➤ **Massage on a neutral leather cream or cleaner.** This restores softness and sheen without changing the color. Always test first in a discreet spot. Be extra wary of colored bags and shoes, which can run or stain when dampened. I've used Nivea face cream or plain coconut oil in a pinch, and window cleaner on patent leather, but, again, test first! Gently rub the cream or cleaner into the

> ## Treat leather bags and shoes like you do your own skin. They need consistent moisturizing…

Treat leather bags and shoes like you do your own skin. They need consistent moisturizing to stay supple and prevent cracking or peeling, filler to stuff and preserve shape, pro repairs, and "makeup" to fix damage due to age, wear, and weather.

➤ **Buff off dust first with a soft cloth.** Pay attention where the leather meets the sole on shoes and seams of bags, and use a clean toothbrush to lift out dirt where it's trapped. Brush suede shoes and boots with a hard toothbrush.

leather item (shoe, bag, belt, boot) with a soft, clean cloth. You won't believe how it blends away scratches and renews that just-bought finish.

➤ **Be proactive.** Find a good local shoe repair shop and get replacement lifts for heel bottoms before they wear down to the nails. Once they do the damage is irreparable. Take new shoes and boots in and ask for a thin layer of rubber to be added to the soles before wearing. Buy a water-proofing spray and mist newbies lightly from 6 inches away. And if you must wear real pumps in the pouring rain, stick to patent leather since the varnish adds extra protection.

10 MAKE AN EFFORT TO LOOK GREAT EVERY DAY BECAUSE YOU NEVER KNOW.

Tabloid photos of celebs bare-faced in "off-duty" clothes are one of our biggest guilty pleasures! Our mothers warned us to always look good (and wear nice underwear) long ago. Who at 50 hasn't let the boundaries of comfy and sloppy slip? One minute you're picking up dog food in old sweatpants, a stained tee, and ratty hair and the next you run into a work colleague or your ex (and his new "friend") in the parking lot. Show and tell is not on our fun list. Celebs get public redemption with hundreds of glam shots of their diva selves. Not us! That blotchy face, saggy skipped-the-bra chest, and oversize Springsteen tee are all people remember.

Cheat life's curveballs with a beauty blast and ready-to-go uniform for quickie dashes. It makes the difference between icky and incredible, embarrassment and envy.

Just slap on a shimmery tinted moisturizer, a rosy lip balm, mist your roots with dry shampoo or do a ponytail, spritz on perfume, add sunglasses, slip into your boob-hiking everyday bra, a simple V neck sweater or plain white tee, your favorite jeans, good flats. Done and out the door!

SASS TALK: WHEN IS A SPLURGE WORTH IT? OR NOT!

We've learned to wait for sales on big-ticket items; shop trendy, low-cost chains like Zara, Urban Outfitters, and H&M for cheap chic; check discount sites like bluefly.com, farfetch.com, and theoutnet.com; and seek salon, spa, and restaurant deals on Groupon. But every woman has an urge to splurge in her DNA. Only you know what triggers yours. "Is that worth it?!" you wonder. Should you click "Buy," stall and click "Save for Later,"or dump it in "Shopping Cart"? This is the modern predicament for shopping and life itself as we ponder every move. So I ask:

Is buying a French Diptyque candle for $60 nuts when I can get a scented candle for $15? No . . . because it makes me feel like I'm living in Paris when I'm really hunkered down working at home in a New York suburb.

Is a $50 designer lipstick worth the packaging when a similar shade and texture lie in wait at the drugstore for $8? Not for me and my skinny, nearly nonexistent lips. When to go for it and when to show restraint varies woman to woman. In this book I present my friend Carol, who had no problem snapping up faux leather pants from Walmart's junior department for $8. The fact that she always wears them with a $590 Louis Vuitton scarf and $1,000 Prada boots is irrelevant. For Carol all three items were equally worth it and make her feel good. Money is a big issue these days but "splurge" doesn't always mean dollar signs. Sometimes "splurge" means instant gratification like taking a "sick" day off from work to watch Netflix. A splurge is when something in our psyche is saying "green light!"

JUST BETWEEN US: 10 WISE WOMEN TRUTHS TO SMILE ABOUT

Back in the day we'd be revered as sages for our insights and plain-old common sense. When we're with peers we nod knowingly as the media makes proclamations: navy is the new black! Duh, navy is never "out" and it's always been great *with* black. Tell us something we don't know!

CAROL E. CAMPBELL

My motto is "Just do it!" I want that slogan on my (God forbid) gravestone! But what is *it*? The problem is identifying what you really want and what is feasible based on your responsibilities as an "older" person. You know what you're good at and you should know what you're bad at. I think transition is about looking at what your true skills are and what your real personal interests are and combining them.

1 WHAT'S IN TODAY WILL BE OUT TOMORROW, THEN IN AGAIN FOR SURE.

Fashion is rarely really new. Inspired by the far past and recent "vintage" (our Hippie, Mod, Disco, Power, and Punk leftovers), designers keep churning out oldies. There's always a new twist. For years tees were *the* basic and then suddenly shirts returned to nudge them out of first place. Worn more casually this time around—untucked or rumpled, sleeves rolled, unbuttoned to a deep V, shirts added a feminine but unstuffy wink to jeans and work clothes. Don't look at "trends" with jaded eyes. Keep them and your fashion options wide open!

2 MAGNIFYING MIRRORS AND GLASSES ARE THE SECRET OF THE UNIVERSE.

It doesn't matter if you've had Lasik surgery, wear glasses, or have near-perfect eyesight naturally. We all need a 10x magnifying makeup mirror on a stand now.

The mirror ensures your eyeliner sits close to the roots of your lashes, mascara isn't clumpy, brows are defined and filled, foundation and eye shadow are well blended.

It's also useful for applying face creams and masks, covering hormonal zits, brown spots, and broken capillaries accurately, and for precision tweezing of stray hairs. The magnifying glass is great for reading teeny print on skincare/haircare labels and product instructions (now that they come in 25 languages in itsy-bitsy type), searching your dog for ticks, to detangle fine necklace chains, remove splinters, do a pedicure, and locate dropped contact lenses and earring backs.

JEANNINE SHAO COLLINS

Change is less scary when you are 50 versus 30. I embrace it with a sense of humor, more resilience, confidence, and a great sense of excitement. What's important is that I'm always learning and surprised how I grow with every turn in my career. Coming back to *MORE* as publisher has been wonderful. I can apply all that I've learned about new media, take risks, and try things that haven't been done before as the magazine evolves.

3 SIMPLE, CHEAP SOLUTIONS ARE OFTEN THE BEST, AREN'T THEY?!

I'm not a big fan of homemade beauty treatments— we're not chemists and inexpensive drugstore ones have all the bells and whistles we need straight from the safety testing of the lab. It's nice to repurpose things, though. Here are my favorite multifunctional items:

➤ **A hinged can opener** gets nasty drugstore makeup plastic blister packs (yes, these are still a problem) open without breaking your nails or wrecking your manicure.

➤ **A lint roller** cleans out the crumbs and crud at the bottom of your handbags fast.

➤ **Candlesticks** make amazing bracelet stackers.

➤ **An Altoids tin** makes a great mini-case for credit card, lipstick, and a key to stash in your coat pocket.

➤ **A rubber band** looped through the buttonhole and around the button will expand your jeans or pant waistband an inch on "bloat" days.

➤ Stuff **scented dryer sheets** in stinky shoes and carry-ons to destroy odors.

➤ Use **nail polish** to ID or code keys, electronic toothbrushes, and chargers.

4 WE WON'T AGE LIKE OUR MOTHERS.

This is usually true unless we smoke, diet, and tan like they did . . . *if* they did. Hopefully we started wearing sunscreen, working out, eating healthy, maintaining a stable weight, practicing smart skincare and haircare early enough to counteract all of the above *even if* mom got you going on ciggies, deprivation, and sunning. Mom missed the boat on sweets and wine, though—we know dark chocolate and a glass of red wine have a beneficial antioxidant kick (just don't overdo it!). Of course, with preventative care and a little dermatological assistance, the looks gap between us and our daughters has narrowed. Take a glance at Kate Hudson and Goldie Hawn, Kris Jenner and Kim Kardashian, Demi Moore and Rumer Willis, Susan Sarandon and Eva Amurri, Melanie Griffith and Dakota Johnson.

5 OUR OLD-SCHOOL HAIR TRICK STILL WORKS.

We always knew rollers and bonnet hair dryers were going to save us someday again. Our chemically processed hair and ache-y arms need a break. Head to your local beauty supply shop or go to sallybeauty.com online and buy a hard-shell egg-shaped bonnet dryer (yes, like the ones salons used to use but portable) or a soft bonnet ionic dryer, that folds into a compact carrying case and rollers. Hair dries in half the time with less concentrated heat and no tension on the hair shaft. Just dry sections of damp hair in Velcro rollers and slip on the hood and you'll have hands free to text, make calls, read, shop online, work at home, or do your makeup! It's what celeb stylists do behind the scenes on shoots to save time and damage.

6 FORGET WHAT MAGAZINES SAY. WE WILL ALWAYS NEED THESE 5 THINGS.

▶ **Mesh fine-gauge fishnet tights in "nude"** because we're not falling for that naked-legs-in-winter idea again, dislike nude sheers, and don't always have time or the inclination to self-tan. The best: Wolford and Commando are worth the splurge.

▶ **Supersoft long scarves** because they style up everything, save us in chilly weather and air-conditioning, and look way cooler than a shawl!

▶ **A crisp white shirt** freshens tired skin and any basic—jeans, a tailored skirt, or black pants—in a blink.

▶ **New slim jeans** with some stretch and a mid-rise of about 8 inches that are narrow but not legging-tight. Roll or crop them at the ankle (if they're not already) or wear them long and lean. No tugging the waistband up every time you sit down and stand up!

▶ **Lightweight cashmere pullovers and cardigans** are classy, sexy, and make us feel "rich." Choose slouchy pullovers, fitted bateau and V-necked sweaters, and long V-neck cardigans with pockets in your favorite neutrals and "happy" colors. The best low-cost cashmeres are online at Uniqlo, so stock up!

7 OILS WORK AND *ALWAYS* MAKE US FEEL SEXY.

Oils are the real reason we love spa treatments and facials. The whole massage and glow aspect is catnip. My idea of a mini-splurge are the glam DIY "oils" from brands like Josie Maran, Moroccanoil, and L'Oréal Paris Age Perfect for their delish argan oil and blends of essential oils. Packed with essential fatty acids, antioxidants, and vitamins, they nourish and restore mature skin and hair as an alternative or supplement to your usual treatments for face, hair, and body. A pre-bed facial or body oil massage improves radiance, restores dry skin, soothes away a headache, stress, and achy muscles. Purists can try sweet almond oil, apricot kernel oil, or coconut oil from the health-food store, or olive oil (straight from the kitchen) works but is a little salad-y. And sample the divine-smelling jasmine, lavender, and rose oils at Whole Foods while pretending to look for probiotics, vitamins, and protein bars. I do!

8 MULTITASKING IS US... TO A DEGREE.

We're the original jugglers, who spent years balancing work, family, our social life, exercise, and errands like circus performers. Then along came technology to make our lives easier. We're still multitasking, only now we do it on cells, iPads, laptops, apps, and devices that allow us to juggle *more* things *simultaneously.*

We can e-mail a friend, text our kid, read a document from our lawyer, and pay our electric bill while walking on a desk treadmill.

We can participate in meetings while texting other attendees (undetected) to request they voice an opinion, second ours, or shut up . . . and buy a pair of readers online, too, during lulls in the conversation. We download apps, create playlists, find *those* great booties discounted, and gain control over our bodies and weight by counting calories eaten or burned. Technology simplifies multitasking but don't be so busy on your iPhone and tablet that you miss the joy of being somewhere, with someone, and living. OKAY?!

9 REPETITION IS GOOD, NEW IS BETTER.

Reinforcing our memory with lists, puzzles, a blog diary, books, smells, routines, and music we love is healthy, whether we're following a recipe we know by heart, doing our usual makeup, or sudoku online. It keeps that knowledge alive.

But when we do something we've never done before we're challenging our brains to stimulate the formation of new cells and help reduce cognitive decline.

For example, learn how to play the guitar or violin (you don't have to be Sheryl Crow or Anne-Sophie Mutter—just *try*), how to set up and operate a computer and get on all social media without a teenager, how to foster a Seeing Eye puppy until it's ready for formal training (seeingeye.org). New is new!

10 STRESS CAN MAKE US BREAK OUT... EVEN AFTER 50!

Confirmed! It's just as we always thought, though hormonal changes do play a part. Dr. Debra Jaliman says, "Stress *can* contribute to breakouts. Also some medications such as lithium, steroids, phenytoin (Dilantin for seizures); certain vitamins such as B2, B6, and B12; and some medical problems like polycystic ovary syndrome can cause senior acne."

"Most women can't believe it when blemishes start appearing alongside their wrinkles and saggy skin. Remember retinol and BHAs treat acne as well as aging skin as double-duty products."

For women who had acne as teens and are seeing a resurgence, Dr. Jaliman says, "See your dermatologist ASAP. Prescription products that help both acne and aging like Ziana Gel, Retin-A, and Retin-A Micro at the low concentration of 0.04 percent are helpful, too."

BROADMINDED:
HOW TO LOOK AMAZING ON SOCIAL MEDIA, BECAUSE YUP... YOU NEED TO!

Your tweets may be brilliant, your e-mails sparkling, but if you don't look good on LinkedIn, Facebook, and Match.com forget it!

CONTROL YOUR PHOTO PLACEMENTS.

Don't use the same photo for a business site like LinkedIn as you do for social and dating sites. People do look you up on multiple platforms. An HR recruiter will check LinkedIn, Facebook, and Twitter—and a potential date will, too.

LOOK SLIMMER EVEN IN A HEADSHOT.

The trick is to push your shoulders down and back while pushing your face forward to tighten your jaw and elongate your neck. Use a "prop" to relax and angle your body. Lean against a wall, doorway or chair, use your pockets, or sit on a stair. Propping your elbow on a table, palm resting on chin for a head-in-hand shot is a classic instant face-lift since it trims and hides the jaw. And remember this isn't a fashion shoot; it's a photo of *you*.

NO HEAD-ON MUG SHOTS FOR CORPORATE OR BUSINESS PHOTOS.

For work sites look super professional and get a studio headshot taken—this is not your best friend's job. Look friendly and businesslike but project personality. Wear a solid color that contrasts against a white or pale gray background.

CONNECT WITH THE VIEWER!

Smile from within so your eyes sparkle and your grin is genuine. Just shake your head to free your hair and give it some separation. That always keeps a photo looking youthful. Think about someone or something you adore—your private crush, a vacation in Mexico. Say peas and carrots to relax your lips.

WATCH THE LIGHTING AND WHERE THE CAMERA IS.

If there's no flash, face the light source head on—it should shine directly on you to blank out lines, wrinkles, and discolorations. Turn your head slightly off center so your good side is toward the camera and light. Selfies for social media look better when you face sunlight, a window, lamp, or streetlight. Keep the camera lens level with your eyes or just above you but focus your eyes just above the camera lens, not into it. Never shoot or let anyone else take a photo from below your eye level. Guaranteed double chin! And if you're shot from too high above, you'll be all nose.

CHAPTER TWO:

REINVENTING WORK

STILL IN THE GAME AND STICKING AROUND FOR MORE.

Who's slacking off? The only "rocker" we'd consider is Mick Jagger. Not one woman I know says she's retired. If we're not working full-time, part-time, or from home, we're volunteering, job hunting, interviewing, taking intern positions to get back in, learning new skills to start over, or "working" as caregivers for grandkids and family members. Though full-retirement age is 66, who ever thinks they have enough money to stop working? What if we live to 100? Or more? And we just might if stats keep rising. Even those of us who made some serious money, married it, nabbed it in a pre-nup or divorce settlement, inherited it, or invested wisely early on aren't sitting around on the beach empty-handed. Even if we *are* lolling around Myrtle Beach, Cape May, or the Hamptons we're blogging, starting our own websites, writing our memoirs, working online for nonprofits, or crafting to sell our pottery, jewelry, or knitwear. Our work ethic is still going strong whether a paycheck is involved or not.

RENE SYLER

I was fired by CBS from my job as cohost of *The Early Show* and have no idea why, even after all these years. I spent four and a half years on the national stage and enjoyed every minute, but I'm not looking in the rearview mirror because it propelled me to my next move. My advice? *All* jobs lack security unless you are working for yourself, which brings with it a whole new set of challenges. Diversify your work portfolio and think of other revenue streams you can pursue while working in your current position. When I started my media brand Good Enough Mother (after my 2007 bestselling book of the same name), I did so in part to share my parenting experiences (as a married, working mom of 2), and establish myself as an expert on a broader platform. I wrote my content for goodenoughmother.com and slowly mastered Facebook, Twitter, Pinterest, LinkedIn, and finally Instagram, and I use all of them to propel my brand.

AGE IS APPROPRIATE AND AWESOME

We know how to power through. At 50, adversity often hits us personally and professionally. We might be caring for a sick partner or aging parent, have family problems, a financial crisis, or our own health concerns. Know what? We still show up. Business as usual. Add work problems to all of the above. Many women 50+ have experienced "restructuring," staff cuts, or a marginalized position when management wants to eliminate their job. So we suck it up and plan our exit strategy like the pros we are. Some HR people think we're overqualified, unable to "fit in" or adapt to new technology-driven workplaces, or that age-related "issues" inhibit productivity. That's BS. We're quick learners, excellent multitaskers, and crisis solvers.

Ageism *is* common, though few employers, managers, HR personnel, or recruiters are willing to admit it for publication.

Many interviewed for this book did, though "off the record." Check out job boards for seniors like AARP's Life Reimagined for Work, powered by LinkedIn, Encore.org, and SimplyHired.com (using its 50+ filter). They can direct you to companies that are 50+ friendly. But, of course, that's only a lead.

Ageism *is* common,
though few are willing to admit it.

JEANNINE SHAO COLLINS

I get a lot of my energy from work. I have not experienced ageism in the workplace but I do have friends who were let go because they make a lot more than their younger counterparts. They have trouble getting back in because of their salary demands and their lack of digital expertise. I say "reinvent yourself." Start your own business if you can...the world always needs innovation.

LET'S DISH

"Let me know when you land" is what people say when you lose your job. It lets the recipient of your news off the hook as they thank God it's not them. Competing with our peers is tough, but competing with Gen Xers and Millennials for jobs can be depressing. Get over it! So they have flawless skin, thick hair, naturally white teeth, and dazzling social media skills. We have flawless résumés, genuine experience (after all anyone can buy great skin, hair, teeth, and tech know-how now), plus dazzling people skills (we're talking actual face-to-face, not online) . . . and we can spell without Google.

BUT YOU, MY FRIEND, HAVE AN EDGE WAY BEYOND THAT, SO LISTEN UP:

Detail how you enhanced profits. As the original workaholics, we organized life around work. We climbed our way up the ladder in heels, paid our dues, and instead of reaping our rewards, we're still working! Stop saying you have excellent communication or management skills. All anyone cares about is the bottom line. Money. In interviews and at work, be ready to spew exact stats. For example, if you increased profits by 40 percent, say so and explain exactly how you did it. If you always came in under budget by 25 percent, say so and explain why and how you did so while increasing those profits. Your precise numbers count more than your former big macher title now.

EMPHASIZE YOUR FLEXIBILITY AND AVAILABILITY.

Younger workers put family first. All those weekend soccer games, basketball coaching, extended family vacations, cocktail marathons with work chums, nanny or daycare problems leave them exhausted. We're energized! So we can take on their projects midstream, step in for women on maternity leave, and we don't mind working overtime (or the pay plus salary).

NETWORK TO DEATH.

Remember you've still got what it takes. A quickie class to fine-tune your computer skills, learn the most current programs, and step up your social media never hurts. Call every lead and cold-call companies to ask for an interview, too. What are 30 years of guts for? You just might start your own Fortune 500 company if you try.

....

Q: Colleagues say I remind them of
their mother. Harassment?!

A: Take it as a compliment!
Most moms 50+ rock, just say "thanks!"

I'm not a job counselor or life coach but I do know in the end, appearance counts. When job hunting it may get your L.K.Bennett-shod foot through the door and, if you are working keep it there. Looking good makes you stand out in a meeting or large workplace and adds that extra push for a promotion or bonus. You shouldn't look like you're trying to be your 25- or 35-year-old self. Get inspiration by Googling top women fashion designers who are in their 50s, 60s, and even 70s, like Donna Karan, Nanette Lepore, Nicole Miller, Catherine Malandrino, and Carolina Herrera. See how they adapt trends to suit their bodies and personal style. Diane von Furstenberg is clearly as contemporary in dress and attitude as the models who walk her runway, but you'd never say she's trying to look 25!

Age doesn't affect her choices—her preferences and attitude does. Women in fashion know their "look" by 50 and you do, too. So dress *up* for work whether you're the CEO or a worker bee in a big machine. It boosts your self-esteem and image. Even working from an office over your garage, in a small local business, or part-time, stay super groomed—manicured nails, glossy healthy-looking hair, and well-cared-for skin that shouts, as L'Oréal Paris says it so well, "I'm worth it!"

....

BEEN THERE, DONE THAT

I started freelance life missing the collaborative buzz of a full-time job. The Starbucks-fueled brain-storming, the routine, my personal staff, the wacky camaraderie, and even the bitchy backstabbing of office politics in publishing. It was powerful fuel. I was used to being a diva, a leader, a workaholic, and I loved it. But then I learned to like my new-found freedom even better. Working from home in my favorite jeans I could adjust the heat and air-conditioning to my hot and cold flashes, choose how to spend my time and be super-selective about projects and clients. Best of all, I could make more money doing less and become my own brand instead of building someone else's. But even working freelance, it's critical to stay motivated, adapt to industry changes, and continue to reach out to new contacts, suggest new assignments or projects, and never disengage from clients and colleagues—congratulate them on promotions or job changes. Stay in the loop.

NANCY GANZ STEIR

My parents were in the fashion business, so I learned all about manufacturing and design from them. I went out on my own with the Nancy Ganz line of sportswear and dresses and then a few years later, in 1989, created Hipslips to go under fitted dresses for a smoother look. I trademarked the name and included them free with every shipment. Soon after the intimate apparel buyers were knocking down my showroom doors. Realizing this was the way to go, I closed my fashion company and founded Bodyslimmers by Nancy Ganz in 1990 with the Hipslip as the basic must-have, but that soon expanded to thighslimmers and bellybusters. In 1996 I closed an amazing deal with Warnaco and sold the brand. I get asked how I feel about Spanx, which was founded in 2003. I never regretted my decision to sell and I think Spanx has done an awesome job. I'm not at all surprised that shapewear has become a booming business.

LOIS'S TUTORIAL OF TRICKS #2

WE GET IT! 10 INSIDER TIPS EVERY WORKING B-BABE SHOULD KNOW

Let's say you've been working since college. The who, what, where of your work have evolved and so have your needs, values, and standards. We've changed and so has the way women work.

1 DON'T WEAR A SUIT—ONLY CIA AGENTS, FOREIGN MINISTERS, HIGH-PROFILE LAWYERS, AND POLITICIANS DO.

Even Michelle Obama; Mindy Grossman, CEO of the Home Shopping Network; Desirée Rogers, CEO of Johnson Publishing Company; and *Vogue* editor Anna Wintour go everywhere in dresses. Suits feel stuffy but dresses get the combo of style, speed, and professionalism right. If you have the dough,

serious work ethic message without giving up style or personality.

Dresses are our emergency exit door from the playground-world of fashion trends. No tricky pieces to put together, just instant polish. Five tips are all you need:

> [A tailored dress gives women 50+ body confidence]

make one dress a year an investment splurge—expensive, perfectly tailored, and in a pricey fabric. This is like buying a new sofa or a dining table—you want to love it and make it last. It'll provide an ego boost and impress the hell out of colleagues, your boss, and clients.

A tailored dress gives women 50+ body confidence and is the new work uniform that sends a

> **Sheaths, Shifts, and Fit and Flare.** These 3 major dress shapes show your shape or disguise it, depending on style. Sheaths skim curves and suit women of any size with total body confidence—show-offs welcome! Shifts are cut straighter and sleeker and have a modern, minimalist look. They blur body contours and hide a waist MIA or a flabby middle. Fit and flare dresses define your

KEEP REFERENCES CURRENT...
which is why you need to eavesdrop.
Listen to and get inspired by how younger
people phrase things (without using
obvious street slang).

upper body until the waist, then let go in an A-line. They look sleek on top and give hips, thighs, and derriere plenty of wiggle room.

➤ **Necklines matter, hemlines, too.** Avoid showing cleavage or too much back. It's not businesslike. Choose higher necklines like slash, boat, crew, ballet, shallow scoops, and wide discreet Vs. Dress length at 50 depends on your dress, shape, personal style, and workplace. However, most women look best in a just-top-of-the-knee or an inch-above length.

➤ **Bare arms.** This is our "okay-to-display" zone. Hardly anyone in their 50s and 60s has Madonna-like biceps. Got that? If we do lift weights our upper arms *improve* but we *all* have that little bit of fleshiness—it's normal and womanly. Look at John Singer Sargent's *Portrait of Madame X* for inspiration. Self-tanner can ease discomfort at going sleeveless, but why not just buy sleeves if you're that hung up about it? Dresses with elbow, three-quarter, and long sleeves are all over stores year-round. No more jacket or cardigan obsessions necessary.

2 TALK MORE LIKE GEN XERS AND MILLENNIALS DO.

You don't need to look like them, but you do need to watch your voice and language. Stop saying "I know I sound like a broken record" (they've never seen a record!) or mentioning how you miss typewriters and rotary dial phones with cords, though I kind of do. But be yourself. In some instances, being "retro" is super cool. I drink plain old tap water while younger clients and colleagues look at me in horror as they swig bottled H_2O rattling on about purity and toxins and germs. Ha!

Keep references current, up-to-date, and relevant, which is why you need to eavesdrop. Listen to and get inspired by how younger people phrase things (without using obvious street slang).

Stay on top of cultural events, news, music, fashion, lifestyle trends, TV shows, movies, and technology so you can contribute to daily chitchat knowingly. Of course, we're more interested in things like how our stocks are doing, if the government will shut down, the results of our bone density test, and whether we should continue taking a daily baby aspirin. But having a Twitter handle, knowing who Katniss is, what Nicki Minaj and Kim Kardashian have in common, and being able to recognize and sing lyrics from people like Lorde, Haim, and Taylor Swift count. Sorry.

3 MARKET YOUR AGE AS A BONUS. DON'T EVER APOLOGIZE FOR IT.

Treat younger people—boss, coworkers, or personal assistant—as peers. Clearly it's illegal for anyone to ask about your age but HR might say, "How would you feel working for someone a lot less experienced than you?" Clever B-Babes respond:

> **Emphasize your knowledge and problem-solving skills.** If you've been out of work for a year or made heaps more money than the salary offered, you're seen as a risk. Underline you don't need training or hand-holding to step in and do the job on day one.

> [I think of experience as an ongoing process, so I'm always learning.]

"I think of experience as an ongoing process, so I'm always learning. I've had coworkers with different backgrounds, expertise, and insights—and it was an asset. They boosted my own abilities."

> **Make stress work for you.** A manager might ask, "You know this is a high-speed, high-pressure industry?" Say, "Good question. Stress is the new 'normal' in all workplaces, so I've learned to assess and prioritize what needs to be done first and what can be done quickly but well." Finis!

> **Keep it friendly and generous . . . on your end.** Some colleagues are genuinely interested in our knowledge and impressive work history; others just feel threatened by it. We spent decades dealing with office politics and know people are only interested in what we can do to help them.

> **Get compensated fairly.** Know what the job pays. If it's a choice between no work and getting the job, grab the job. You can always renegotiate when you've proven yourself invaluable.

BRENDA COFFEE

I work at home and I'm very disciplined. Ageism and sexism still comes into play. I met some real jerks when I was raising start-up capital for 1010 Park Place. A prospective investor asked me if women over 40 know how to use a computer. My favorite was the guy who said, "We like to invest in sexy deals and there's nothing sexy about women over 45." I wanted to say, "I know your wife. Does she realize you feel this way?" I'd start a doggie day care before I took a job I hated or one where I wasn't appreciated.

4 IF YOU'RE THE BOSS, BE A MENTOR.

Your staff has different goals than you did. Younger women now try to blend their work and social lives as much as possible. Raised in the speedy social media age, they expect rapid salary and title upgrades just for doing the job—not as we did by going above and beyond. Use those with show-y tech skills to your advantage by rewarding them with new coaching responsibilities. Keep full-time staff on their toes with eager interns, too. But draw the line at what to wear, some Millennials and Gen Xers have no idea what "appropriate" work wear means.

As a manager it's okay to inform employees of the actual dress code if they get too sloppy, bare, provocative, or come to work in gym clothes . . . just do it in a professional way via an all-inclusive memo, not one-on-one.

And, of course, they don't have to mimic your own style, but the clever ones will.

5 USE SOCIAL MEDIA AS A TOOL, NOT A TIME-FILLER.

We spend extensive time online. It's become our top source of info and how-to-do-anything resource, leaving little time to actually *do* anything else. If your inbox is clogged, unsubscribe from sales alerts, restrict check-ins of anything but work e-mails to once a day, same for Facebook feed. Pay more attention to your LinkedIn account and fast-track connections to the right people.

➤ **Be assertive and ask for introductions.** Say exactly why you're reaching out. Once connected, tell them how they can help—industry advice or assistance with a specific job opening, for example.

➤ **Then supplement online intros via e-mail and phone.** Get personal. People respond if you can get hold of their e-mail address, assistant's e-mail, or direct office number or cell.

6 BE CAREFUL ABOUT WHAT YOU POST AND WHERE.

Use LinkedIn to build business contacts. Don't automatically connect to your real estate agent, your accountant, or your eye doctor "to be nice" if they don't fit the work criteria. Assume everything is public. You never want to get tagged on Facebook or snapped for someone's Instagram feed looking tired and disheveled, and those quick micro-blog "tweets" can bite you in the derriere. Think of yourself as a politician.

7 IF YOU WORK AT HOME AND NEVER SEE ANOTHER SOUL, GET DRESSED FOR IT.

Your "looks" show up in your voice and come across as confident.

Sloppy dress habits spill over into your work attitude and before you know it . . . you're shopping online. Your "looks" show up in your voice and come across as confident on conference calls. Place your desk near a window to maximize daylight or use mirrors to brighten and enlarge the space. When you do have in-person meetings "outside" with clients, dress as they do—depending whether the environment is corporate, creative, or polished but casual.

8 BE GOOGLE-ABLE.

We have a work history, accomplishments, and a brain still on fire with deep personal interests. We all have imaginary products, business ideas in our heads, and dream about *Shark Tank* investors lunging at us in joy. Or actually getting the initial round of funding on Kickstarter. While most of us won't go this far, starting your own business is possible.

➤ **Create your own website or blog.** Let's say you were a school librarian but have an extensive knowledge of history and travel especially in Southeast Asia. You might start by creating a website and blog about your travels there.

➤ **Use social media to promote yourself.** Then use Facebook, Instagram, Twitter, and Pinterest to promote your blog and provide a voice and image.

➤ **Work it.** You might snag work part-time for a travel agency or as a "guide" on tours to Southeast Asia and then launch your own business coordinating historical tours for seniors.

KAREN OLIVER

Women 50+ grew up in an age when building contacts and forging strong relationships could only be accomplished via face-to-face interactions—so there we really do have an advantage over younger women. When I am pitching a new client, I always prefer to do it in person, to connect on a human level—which for me is the key to developing a long-lasting alliance. I started out in the beauty business at I. Magnin, selling Erno Laszlo cosmetics behind the counter, and went on to work on amazing brands including Lancôme, Borghese, Shiseido, Dior, and Helena Rubinstein, where I was a VP. I've worked really hard to live my life in the moment and feel as if I'm living my dreams. I've found you can learn something from everyone, regardless of age. There will always be someone smarter, younger, and prettier than you, so focus on what makes you unique and special. And remember that experience is valuable—an advantage that comes with age.

9 MAKE YOUR BRAIN STRESS-CONTROL HQ.

We avoid burnout by resetting our perspective and shaking off negativity. It's a learned discipline. There are some things we can control, others we can't. Learn to say no (to the endless flow of pop-ins, e-mails, texts, and phone calls) and add down-time for yourself. Asking for a raise always pushes stress buttons. So when you do:

➤ **Do your research** before having that difficult conversation. Ask a successful colleague *you trust*—for guidance.

➤ **The actual raise discussion** should include a reasonable but challenging base salary, bonuses, and equity. Have in mind acceptable non-financial compensation if your company can't come through. You might suggest extra vacation days or working remotely one day a week.

➤ **Always pump up the salary number** you're asking for so there's room to negotiate—keep it on the high end of realistic.

➤ **Don't answer work e-mails on weekends**—your off-duty time is exactly that. Who needs work-prompted insomnia, eating binges, eczema, anxiety, elevated blood pressure, a heart attack, or stroke? Not us!

10 BE KIND TO THOSE WHO ARE UNEMPLOYED OR UNDEREMPLOYED.

If it's you, stay steady. Your everyday work "friends" often dry up like yesterday's nonfat muffin. Losing your jobs reveals who your real work chums are. Every woman 50+ ever let go says the same thing.

True buds will: help enlist a good age discrimination lawyer if necessary, listen to the initial ranting and cursing, provide a temporary "nest" with them until we rally, and not let life trickle to pretend conversations with Kathie Lee and Hoda each a.m.

Great friends will not allow you to slink quietly into the blues or wallow in self-pity. When I left magazine publishing, my best friend Charla marched me out of the building and straight into a celebratory lunch. She sent me a makeup bag that said "Queen of the F*#_king World!" We're all tackling the same crap life hurls our way. Never look back.

SASS TALK: DON'T REPLICATE YOUR OLD JOB EVER AGAIN!

Let it go. You can't recreate your old life, career, salary, relationships, marriages, friendships, and certainly you can't bring back at 50 or 60 the job you had at 35, so stop trying. Find out where the hot jobs for women your age are. Do something entirely new if it comes down to that. Maybe you'd be great as: an assisted living specialist, physical therapist, convention and event planner, or dog walker. Look into business services like bookkeeping, IT, working as an interpreter, or translator. Some jobs require certification but not a bachelor's degree if you're concerned about student loans again. Check AARP.org for up to the minute info on jobs and re-careering.

Thanks to early mentoring by heavy hitters like Gloria Steinem and Betty Friedan, we are expert negotiators who have developed an extra gene that allows us to change husbands, wrinkle creams, and jobs with equal gusto.

Here's what I know: make a list of the jobs you'd kill for, the could-do-blindfolded jobs you're qualified for, and the "okay, whatever" jobs that are in sync with your know-how but have nothing to do with your previous work history. Call friends of friends, relatives of friends, friends of relatives, alumni associations, college and university placement offices, local community centers, hospitals, and local government offices, and stay open to anything.

JUST BETWEEN US: 10 ESSENTIALS WORKING WOMEN 50+ BETTER HAVE

You could have the creative chops and money-making instincts of an Oprah Winfrey or Sheryl Sandberg and it wouldn't matter. Your résumé is the #1 must-have but packaging is the other 90 percent of it. So here's your checklist in order of importance:

> We have developed an extra gene that allows us to change husbands, wrinkle creams, and jobs with equal gusto.

1 A CONCISE CURRENT RÉSUMÉ.

It's really all about the interview when it comes to getting the job, but you need the résumé to initiate that face-to-face interview. Keep it simple, clear, and precise:

➤ **Choose a classic font, black type, white paper,** no photo, bolding, or underlining. One or two pages only.

➤ **List your most recent or present job first and go backward over the last ten years,** but don't go past that no matter how many years you've worked.

➤ **Give your position at the companies you've worked for** (including what they do since that might not be obvious), how long you were there (month and year to month and year), and your accomplishments.

➤ **Briefly summarize work experience prior to ten years but omit dates.** Be smart, don't tell, and they won't ask.

➤ **List your technology skills.** This is important for all—from entry-level to senior management positions. Otherwise it's like showing up in a great party dress with undone hair and makeup.

➤ **Tailor every résumé to the company and position.** Yes, this takes time and homework, but then you're prepared to say how you can help them improve performance—which means knowing how well they're doing and any glitches they're having.

MAURY ROGOFF

I started my own public relations business right out of college and never had a day off—but I did have freedom and power. Technology changed the way I work. With a Blackberry I could be an attentive mother while working full-time. My client contacts and business were in the palm of my hand at a baseball game, a volleyball tryout, in line for school pickup, or in between book and bake fairs. I've kept my passion, curiosity, and interest in my business all these years and I know I'm fortunate.

2 ONE TRULY GREAT BAG AND CLASSY SHOES.

When men "make it," they buy hot sports cars and invest in stocks; when women do, we buy absolutely fantastic shoes and bags. Martha Stewart, the queen of England, and thousands of working women 50+ know a neutral, better-than-average bag, and classy pumps offer instant credibility. Your shoes and bag actually matter more than the clothes. The latter can be from Target, H&M, or the back of your closet, but the accessories better say quality, confidence, and taste.

➤ **Invest in one medium-size all-purpose bag.** You don't need ten low-cost ones. This single luxury item will upgrade everything you wear. Make sure it holds all your stuff, but avoid lugging huge bags—not good for image or posture.

➤ **Designer bags still have clout.** Go to a consignment site like Walk In My Closet or Portero for a gently used Chloé, Hermès, or Chanel. The discount designer The Outnet and eBay are good, too. Plenty of more affordable well-made satchels and shoulder bags for work can be found by Tory Burch, MICHAEL Michael Kors, and Longchamp.

➤ **Buy basic black, brown, and nude shoes.** Beautifully made designer shoes are what online sales are for! You can't miss with elegant pumps (in a heel height you prefer), tapered toe flats, slim ankle boots, booties, and tall classic boots. But don't be afraid to add trendier styles to the mix, too, so long as the quality is there and colors are neutral.

3 DAILY ACCESS TO A TREADMILL.

It's fast and works. Running or fast-walking for 30 minutes on a moving walkway gives you a concentrated bolt of fitness and burns calories. You don't have to worry about avoiding traffic or weather conditions, slipping on black ice, a curb, or crack in the sidewalk the way you do outdoors. If you have room at home, it's a worthy investment for early morning workouts while you catch the news, listen to music, or meditate to start the day. It gives you an instant energy boost and your skin a glow. Just perk up the incline to increase the intensity.

MYRNA BLYTH

I've always loved working and I consider that a great gift. In my 50s, I was running magazines as editor in chief of *Ladies' Home Journal* and *MORE*, which I started in my 60s, and now I am loving my career at AARP. I always wanted to work, write, edit. A writer can always write and work no matter what their age.

4 A CAMERA-READY MAKEUP KIT.

Know how those morning and daytime TV show hosts wear what we'd consider full party makeup? There's a reason for it. The best-kept office secret is how old, drab, and tired women 50+ *who are really attractive in person* look on video conferences in rooms with crappy overhead fluorescent office lighting. Any wrinkles, pigmentation issues, and dryness are amplified onscreen. You need definition, so going a little over-the-top here is okay. Wear:

➤ **A full-coverage semimatte foundation powder** that contains no mica or titanium dioxide (so you don't go ghostly from light reflection).

➤ **Fine-tip black or brown eye liner** in a high-pigment, long wear roll-up has enough intensity, a controlled line for close to the lashes definition, and smear-proof wear.

➤ **Dense black mascara** opens and emphasize eyes.

➤ **Cream blush** in a sheer bright shade high on the cheeks.

➤ **A hybrid lip liner/color** in a creamy matte—like L'Oréal Paris Le Matte Velvety Full Cover Lip-Colour or Maybelline Color Blur by Lip Studio—gives lasting shape and color on camera.

➤ **False lashes,** if you can handle them.

ALISON HOUTTE

When my modeling career of the '80s started fading, I reinvented myself with my vintage clothing store, Hooti Couture. Money was very tight in our family of 6 kids growing up in Florida, so at a young age I was introduced to garage sales, flea markets, and thrift shops. I learned how to look good on a few bucks and my grandma, Hooti, and mom, Jackie, taught me it's okay to be different. When Hooti Couture (a play on Haute Couture and Grandma Hooti) was born I decided to fill the shop with clothing and accessories I really loved and keep it full of fun, eclectic clothes. I've worked my tail off for the last 19 years and love my shop but I'm getting priced out of a very "hot" neighborhood in Brooklyn so another transition is coming.

5 WORK—FACE BOTOX.

Botox is so worth it for job hunting and keeping. The 11s—those etched-in-place vertical furrows between the brows can make us look angry, hostile, depressed, scary, and unapproachable. Choose a board-certified dermatologist or cosmetic surgeon who specializes in Botox (botulinum toxin). She'll inject the muscles, causing these lines to deactivate, and you go straight back to work. Anywhere from 2 days to a week later, a smooth forehead emerges and stays for 3 months or longer.

6 THE RIGHT HAIR COLOR.

[Hair color is one of the first things people notice.]

If your hair color looks frankly fake, is too dark, or washes you out, forget about that new dress. Haul your derriere to a salon and get highlights ASAP for the fastest fix. They will improve any hair color instantly. Then discuss further changes.

Whether you make a 180-degree color change, go brighter, lighter, or just add highlights—hair color is one of the first things people notice.

Does gray hair affect work ability? No, it doesn't. If you own your business, work from home, or have a huge power position . . . it's safe to go for it (see Chapter One for how-to); otherwise, think twice. How many female TV anchors, celebs over 50, and Fortune 500 CEOs are gray? So far hardly any. A few women have that pale gray-blonde hue that makes it hard to tell what's going on but that's about it. It might be financially smarter to keep the blonde, brunette, or red gig going.

7 A SMILE MAKEOVER.

A bright white, even set of teeth creates a healthy, youthful look, but the right cosmetic dental work can do even more. Just getting your old dark fillings replaced with tooth-color resin and whitening treatments or at-home strips can take years off your mouth. According to cosmetic dentist Dr. Marc Lowenberg of Lowenberg, Lituchy & Kantor in NYC, "On a job interview your teeth have an immediate impact on the way people perceive you." Porcelain veneers have worked for most of the CEOs I talked to—here's why:

➤ **Veneers make teeth look brand-new.** Says Dr. Lowenberg: "Great veneers are translucent, with a soft natural white color and a high glaze. They correct dark-stained, crooked, or short teeth and also expand the arch of your teeth to widen your smile." This adds fullness to lips that have thinned and lost definition, restores teeth to a youthful longer length, and decreases smoker's wrinkles around the upper lip. They're expensive but they last 10 to 15 years. Even doing the front 4 or 6 teeth over makes a huge difference if your teeth are short or jagged. Veneers won't respond to bleaching, so bleach the teeth you are not doing them on before getting the veneers and aim for a shade that blends.

➤ **They give a non-surgical lift.** Veneers plump up your cheeks with extra support at the sides and minimize the nasal labial crease from nose to mouth.

➤ **New procedures are fast and require very little prep.** "Veneers now typically take 2 office visits with very little or no tooth preparation," according to Dr. Lowenberg.

8 A NEW POWER LOOK.

Dresses rule but they're just *part* of your work image. Create a look—just like actors for a TV role. Look at Julianna Margulies and Christine Baranski as hot-shot attorneys on *The Good Wife*, Robin Wright as First Lady on *House of Cards*, Viola Davis as a lawyer and professor on *How to Get Away with Murder*, and Bebe Neuwirth as chief of staff on *Madam Secretary*. It's time to dial up the style. In addition to those do-everything dresses, add tailored pieces like silk blouses, well-made button-down shirts, slim pencil skirts, slim pants, and jackets. Statement necklaces, bold reading glasses, and heels are crucial props and so is perfect hair and big-deal eye makeup. Looking womanly has power. It just might get you a nicer cubicle, a bigger office, or an offer you can't refuse.

9 A PERFORMANCE-BOOSTING SCENT.

Fragrance can enhance your workday. Certain notes can ease a high-tension day, get you going after a sleepless night, or improve your stick-to-it attitude on deadline. Here are the ones that do with fragrances to match:

➤ **Vanilla** is a mood elevator (Shalimar by Guerlain, Prada Candy).

➤ **Jasmine** eases the blues (Tom Ford Jasmin Rouge, Aerin Ikat Jasmin).

➤ **Lavender** (Serge Lutens Encens et lavande) and the smell of **green apples** (DKNY by Donna Karan Be Delicious) calm you down.

➤ **Peppermint** (Commes des Garçons Sherbet Series 5 Peppermint) improves work performance and concentration.

➤ **Citrus** (Tory Burch for Women by Tory Burch, Hermès Eau de Pamplemousse Rose) energizes and gives you a push when working late.

➤ **Spices** like cinnamon pepper, and nutmeg (Yves Saint Laurent Opium, Gucci Guilty) increase your attention span.

10 A MINI-MAKEOVER.

Weekends and off-duty days are your chance to get out of a rut. Get suggestions from department-store makeup artists. Let someone else see you with fresh eyes—book a consultation with a new hairstylist, personal shopper, or a brow specialist. Staying contemporary requires frequent updates but enhances your credibility for "current thinking" at work.

BROADMINDED: HOW TO TRAVEL SOLO, SAFELY, AND LOVE IT!

Women 50+ are world-class travelers. Some of us travel for work to meetings, conferences, or major industry events. But lured by the simplicity of cruises or resorts, the adventure of exotic locales, and the cultural benefits of foreign cities, we're setting out solo, too. Airports and global jaunts are the real challenge. We want to feel comfy, with enough polish to confidently demand upgrades (and get them!). Follow my travel tricks.

NO MORE LUGGING BIG BAGS.

One soft-sided carry-on spinner that stuffs easily under seats or in overhead bins is enough if you pack right. Check your flight and airline requirements but include wheels and handle in your measurements to prevent last-minute gate checks and the hideous wait at baggage claim. Beware of new rules. Some expandable bags are too big to fit at their maximum for onboard rules.

Avoid checking pricey logo bags like Louis Vuitton or Gucci. Yes, an obvious designer bag makes a statement, but it also attracts luggage thieves.

A classy color like matte gold or deep green helps you find your bag faster than black. Look for carry-on bags with exterior pockets to make accessing items during flight easy. Keep your ID secure with hidden name-card holders and tape your e-mail address and itinerary to the inside cover of all luggage. Write your destination (or business on return) address in the outer luggage tag. Take an iPhone photo of your bags to assist in recovery. Ditch old airline tags and stickers that confuse handlers and can be misread by scanners.

DONNA BUNTE

I like working as a model in my 50s so much more! Now I feel more respected for my experience and often I'm older than the production team. Older models are not competing with younger women, so we can be ourselves at this point. Some older models have had cosmetic surgery or Botox (which I have not) or spend hours exercising, but I have a family and another business to run so I'm too busy to compare my looks with others. Working with younger models is a treat—they like to hear what I've experienced and know a modeling career is not something to count on past a certain age (though what age is that?).

DRESS COMFY BUT CLASSY.

Look stylish and groomed for long flights, stretches between connections, waits at the gate, security, and, of course, for arrival. You'll get a better seat/room/table/cab and feel A-list confident.

Dress in three layers—a tailored coat, blazer, or a chic trench over a sweater and tee and ankle pants or jeans to travel from cold to hot or vice versa with comfort control.

A tailored top adds an immediate businesslike, elegant attitude. Wear flats for comfort and speed at security.

CARRY YOUR BEST CHIC HANDBAG.

A soft satchel with handles and a shoulder strap, a cross-body bag, or a tote with a top closure leaves hands free for carry-ons and paperwork. They require no supervision or fear of pickpockets. The perfect size will fit your wallet, passport, phone and tablet, an e-reader, glasses, keys, and beauty essentials without bulging or cramming.

ALWAYS ADD AN OVERSIZE LONG SCARF.

It does 5-way duty as fashion statement, soft blanket, makeshift pillow, lumbar support, and face wrap should your seatmate have a cold or for privacy. Germs are a problem. Never use the pillow or blanket provided and use disinfectant wipes and hand sanitizer to wipe down the arm rest, tray table, and for bathroom visits. Wear headphones (ear plugs and an iPod work, too), carry your Kindle, a sleep mask, and wrap up in that scarf. The combo ensures no intrusions.

WEAR A WIRELESS BRA.

Nothing escapes the TSA's metal-detecting powers and security systems—the metal studs on jeans and the metal in your underwire bra can lead to an all-out wanding check. (And breasts swell in the air, so you'll be avoiding discomfort, too!)

EAT MINDFULLY WHILE TRAVELING.

Go for hard-boiled eggs, light cheese wedges, and individual packets of peanut butter to satisfy your cravings for salty and crunchy. A Caesar salad with chicken is okay, just toss the croutons. Protein rather than bloat-boosting carbs or salty chips is the answer.

MAKE ON-BOARD TIME WORK FOR YOU.

Get an aisle or window seat for more space, comfort, and privacy. Drink plenty of water (not alcohol or bloating sodas) in flight and keep applying moisturizer (or a mask), eye cream, and hand cream.

Cabin pressure and re-circulated air suck moisture from your skin, leaving our faces looking drier and more lined than when we boarded!

MOVE AROUND ON BOARD AND WEAR COMPRESSION STOCKINGS.

Avoid wearing tight skinny jeans and knee-high boots. They can cause circulation problems and swelling or even lead to deep vein thrombosis—a blood clot that forms in the lower leg. Stand up, walk back and forth in the aisle, flex your feet, and do stretches in the restroom line. Wear compression stockings carried in pharmacies or try RejuvaHealth (rejuvahealth.com) for knee-highs, tights, pantyhose, and leggings in light, medium, and firm compression.

PLAY IT SAFE.

Respect local customs regarding bare arms and legs and head coverings in Muslim countries. Wear a sports bra to store extra money and a credit card (this is a great tip anytime) and slip on a wedding-ish band ring. Get a flashlight app on your phone but carry a paper map (cells die unexpectedly). Store a copy of your cards, passport, driver's license, and airline tickets in your room/hotel safe and leave one back home with a friend or relative. No real bling, please, and keep pricey iPads out of sight. Stay connected to friends and family on social media—they'll notice if you're MIA.

PACK SMARTER.

Neutral pieces in one basic dark color work 24/7. Just vary the texture. You'll feel thinner, the deep neutral hue won't show stains or wrinkles, and you can always pick up low-cost filler items as you go.

Bring more tops than bottoms—a fresh top is what people notice.

Use statement necklaces and scarves to style them up.

Knits are great for comfort and lightly woven, relaxed tops and tunics work easily over tees and tanks for coverage, style, and warmth.

Roll all and use big Ziploc baggies to keep things organized and dry, since sitting on the tarmac in rain or snow can cause leaks in even the best luggage.

MULTITASK BEAUTY.

Stockpile samples from department stores and magazine ads. These one-use disposable minis and foil packets of creams, serums, foundation, scent, and creams are ideal travelers. Then multitask:

Use **disposable wipes** to remove face and eye makeup. Those by Neutrogena and Aveeno work best and don't dry out in the soft-side package.

Dry shampoo as a freshener, blowout extender, and volumizer. Look for mini travel sizes.

Tinted moisturizer/BB/CC cream with sunscreen to hydrate, enhance skin tone, nourish, and protect. My favorites are Bobbi Brown BB and CC Creams SPF 35 and Laura Mercier Tinted Moisturizer SPF 20.

Bright, creamy lipstick or stain in a red, rosy color to add a "done" look fast;

Chunky eye pencil/shadow for quick definition. Clinique Chubby Sticks and Charlotte Tilbury Color Chameleons never miss.

Do-all balm to nourish and nurture everything from lips to shoe blisters to cuticles and a cold-reddened nose. Try Aquaphor.

CHAPTER THREE:

YOU GOTTA HAVE FRIENDS

THROUGH THICK AND THIN, DIVORCE AND DISASTER, NEW BOOBS AND BOYFRIENDS.

Just to be clear, I don't mean the hundreds of superficial ones on your Facebook page! At 50 we're learning to gracefully edit out friendships-gone-wrong, stick to those who really count, and develop new platonic relationships with a wider, more diverse group of people. We're expanding our boundaries and blurring the borders of friendship to include men and women of all ages, ethnicities, religious and political affiliations, lifestyles, and beliefs. What do we demand from our friends now? Loyalty. Here's what counts: being there no matter what or when, knowing what to say and when to say it, and when it's better to zip your lips and just hug.

MAURY ROGOFF

I have a few friends—a mix of childhood ones, 2 from college, and a handful of others but I've never been one to boast a gaggle of close buddies. With marriage, children, and a business of being social, I didn't go in for after-work "industry events" because I was crunching over my kids' homework and making chicken fingers. As for social media, I have zero interest in sharing about my personal life. However, I am notorious for dropping letters and cards to friends—not just on birthdays but more random and as a sincere outreach.

AGE IS
APPROPRIATE
AND AWESOME

> The luckiest have a crew who challenge our wits, make us laugh, tell us the do-I-look-fat-in-this truth.

It's a myth that women over 50 don't need or want new friends. How many women our age have the same "besties" since high school or even college? Some remained linked through a history of sororities, early adventures (a summer in England studying art history and British men), days hanging out at the beach after school, Mom-dom, or couple-dom life where old friends come in duos. But more than likely, we've picked up friends along the way.

The luckiest have cobbled together a crew who challenge our wits, make us laugh, tell us the do-I-look-fat-in-this truth, and can call anytime day or night for an "I'll be right over" response.

At this stage in life, most of us have had a few jolts. We've moved away from old ties, are widowed, unemployed, separated, or divorced (nothing tells you who your real friends are more than the last 3). Time to make new connections and reboot your social life. If you find yourself talking to your dog or cat more than people, binge-watching TV daily, or spending mindless hours online . . . you need to get a life!

NANCY GANZ STEIR

I am fortunate to have a few great girlfriends, the ones that you don't need to talk with or see often but just really get you and love you for who you are with no judgment of any kind. We keep in touch via e-mail and planned visits with each other. Making new friends is awesome now. I met a few great ones through my involvement with the NYU College of Arts and Science Advisory Board and through the advisory board of the Dubin Breast Center.

LET'S DISH

THE WORD FRIEND COVERS A LOT OF TYPES:

Some women friends are "talkers." They do a monologue and don't let you get a word in. When you do they just roll right on.

Other friends are "gossip girls." They can't wait to trash, fat-shame a girlfriend who has gained some, or pass on the dirt. These bad-mouth babes are actually frenemies (enemies disguised as friends). Delete!

Most revered friends are like Swiss bank vaults. They'd never reveal anything too personal or pass judgment themselves but you can securely tell them your secrets. They are like living diaries . . . when you need to spill.

If you're in a relationship or married now you probably have "couple friends" who really are duos, a two for one. You get together with them as a foursome or in a group of couples for dinners, brunch, and holidays. The tricky part is sometimes you adore one half and dislike the other but you're stuck with both, especially when your partner is a BFF of one half and you're all part of the same clique. Know that divorce is a deal breaker with this kind—they take sides!

By 50, you get to choose the friends you want to keep and let the negative ones and drainers go. Just because friends share a longtime history doesn't mean they are lifelong keepers.

WHAT KIND OF FRIENDS DO YOU HONESTLY NEED *NOW?*

People really do change over time. Is it important to you that friends share your current interests? How about political, social, or religious beliefs? Do you prefer they have a similar lifestyle or standard of living? This may sound crazy but if your chums only eat in 5-star restaurants and you like exploring little, low-cost, hole-in-the-wall joints; if you love Bill Maher's take on politics and your friend is a Megyn Kelly fan and any discussion turns into a fierce argument, can you live with that? If your friend has gone "authentic," let her hair go gray, stopped wearing makeup, became a total vegan and you are a blonde-on-blonde highlights girl, a makeup junkie, and a Paleo diet fan, do you still have enough in common on the inside to stay the course? You need more than nostalgia to sustain a grown-up friendship.

TRY MAKING "OKAY" FRIENDS INTO BETTER ONES.

If your longtime friendship has reached a "blah" state, go off routine and see what happens. Give it one last chance before you hit cancel. First check who's drifting off—you or them—and why? Try to shake up the norm—get them to join a weekly movie club with you and discuss the film over coffee or tea, switch from brunch at the diner with "the girls" every Wednesday to cooking a meal together at home with a new recipe once a week, schedule a girls-only spa weekend or road trip.

JOIN EVERYTHING—
YOU CAN EDIT OUT LATER.

If you're shy it's not easy to be the new girl. Just grit your chompers and do it anyway. Local environmental groups, bird-watching societies, senior cycling or runners clubs, a meditation or yoga group, choirs, and community outreach organizations all provide opportunities for new meet-ups. So do evening classes for adults at the nearby high school, auditing classes at a nearby college, or a book group at the library.

INVITE NEIGHBORS IN FOR DRINKS, WEEKEND BRUNCH, OR COFFEE.

Hardly anyone stays home anymore or gets invitations from strangers, so the novelty and curiosity will be a draw. Age doesn't matter—who cares if they're 20 years younger or older if the conversation is stimulating and you're having a good time? Play old games like Scrabble, charades, or Monopoly over a cup of chai.

DON'T MOVE TOO FAST OR
GIVE AWAY TOO MUCH TOO SOON.

Friendships take time to develop—it's not instant intimacy. Give new acquaintances a trial-run for a bit. If a fresh friend is too needy or reveals personal details that make you uncomfortable, re-evaluate her as a possible crony. Not every new friend candidate will stick.

· · · · · ·

Q: A friend never pays or splits the check, but says "I'll get lunch/coffee next time." Let it slide?

A: Talk about it. How about lunch/coffee at home instead?

In a buddy system, splitting the check is normal. So is offering to pay for parking when you take one car, or alternating who pays for a latte. But when a chum disappears to the ladies' room as you signal for the check and never mentions reimbursing you or even leaving the tip . . . she's not only cheap, she's a coward and certainly not being honest. Avoid letting differences in finances get in the way of friendships.

· · · · · ·

BEEN THERE, DONE THAT

When I married my husband in 2005, both of us were working full-time at our respective editor and dentist jobs in NYC. "Home" for me became the suburban town where he raised his kids and was a pillar of the local A-list golf club. His close friends were and are to this day mostly married guys from the club with wives who had known one another since forever. My own close friends were a very different mix—divorced chums; working women in the beauty, fashion, and publishing worlds; and former boyfriends who had no interest in my new lifestyle. Today my current "true friends" list is pared short and lean, even though my social media presence says otherwise. I do stay in touch with a lot of old friends online, but those I see and talk to daily are a small club of accomplished, funny, super-smart, confident women with the survival skills of a Navy Seal and the patience of Sigmund Freud—like my confidantes Val and Marilyn. My husband, Robert, tops the list, though.

KAREN OLIVER

I do not use the term "friend" lightly. To me, a friend is family. I meet new friends through work mainly since PR is incredibly social, with lots of opportunities to meet interesting people. I look for common values such as working hard, giving back, being real, and curious about life.

LOIS'S TUTORIAL OF TRICKS #3

WE GET IT! 10 BEST FRIENDS EVERY 50+ WOMAN NEEDS

Not to say one friend can't combine the multi-talents listed in this section (since a few of mine definitely do) but here's where we have need-gaps. My BFFs know there is nothing we can't discuss and haven't…from face-lifts to dry vagina, caregiver woes to constipation, boob jobs to hair loss, age discrimination to monster-men we have known and loved. We've lived through one another's breakups, divorces, work crap, and health issues with tears and laughter. We're still laughing and our inside-joke list is still growing. Sometimes younger friends in their 30s and 40s keep you fresh; other times older chums teach you a lot.

My friend Isabelle is 10 years older than I am. When she told me (years ahead) that our pubic hair turns gray, too, it was like getting a spoiler alert (something I never considered before!). Another pal, Sandrine, going through menopause before I did, warned me about night sweats. She'd been waking up in the middle of the night with a drenched nightgown, clammy sheets, and a new younger boyfriend who couldn't understand what was going on. Practically no one can be an all-purpose friend who provides constant empathy, trust, support, information, introductions, shares your rage or glee 24/7, so more than one ally is a good idea. Here are the girlfriends you want:

1 THE COMMON-SENSE CRONY.

Some friends are almost like moms. They tell you the truth for your own good with a track record that's so consistently right, and we listen. She'll haul you to the dermatologist to check that suspiciously large and growing mole above your lips—the one you thought added a Cindy Crawford–like glamour. She'll tell you when your boyfriend's incessant humming, constant e-mail checks, and texting (while with you), and hideous teeth and breath are reasons to toss him. She's the one who will encourage you to purge your closets and pull your life together. Lacking your unrealistic emotional attachments to dated, small, unflattering clothes, hoarded collections of old mugs, vacation T-shirts, and your ex's button-downs helps. A really fearless girlfriend will arrive armed with big trash bags to haul all away to Goodwill.

Thank the friend with guts to throw ten pairs of your old bad-wash, low-rise jeans in the bag for Goodwill and be ruthless with your "maybe keep" pile.

She'll know when you look at a size 2 dress not worn in a decade and say "I'll wear it when I lose the weight," it's a goner.

2 THE FASHIONABLE SHOPPING-MATE.

Obsessive-compulsive shopping is really a team sport.

You need a chum with genuine style chops who will rein in your shopaholic tendencies. She'll always be ready to hit the mall running, say yay or nay to online buys you crave, and vet flash sale sites for you. She's your personal shopper who understands your desires but prevents you from spending like the wife of a Russian oligarch just because it's on sale.

Obsessive-compulsive shopping is really a team sport. Nothing encourages us to buy or not buy like a friend with strong opinions and patience.

I do trust a few girlfriends to never let the fashion editor in me get impractical. I hear a lot of "You have 3 pairs just like those," "Where and when will you wear that?" and "You work from home!" But I'm grateful for their honesty and desire to keep me from personal bankruptcy.

3 A DIET PARTNER WHO KEEPS YOU HONEST.

Women 50+ will talk about weight-loss surgery—lap band, bariatric, or sleeve—like it's no big deal. Actually it is . . . and not for those wanting to lose that last 10 or 20 pounds that arrived with menopause. These procedures are for serious weight loss due to obesity and a body mass index (BMI) of 40+. You'll know if that's you since your doctor will have discussed it during your annual physical. A fitness-savvy pal can be a real trouper—she'll get you back into a healthy diet and gym regimen and keep you there.

One of my best girlfriends purposely buys white jeans a size smaller on sale in January as incentive to lose extra pounds by May. Know what? She always does!

A diet-bud will buy you a Fitbit twin to her own for a daily but competitive pat on the back. She'll lead the way with salmon, soup, or kale salad at lunch (so you can't have a cheeseburger and fries!), motivate you with compliments ("I can't wait to fit back into my skinny jeans, too!"), and encourage you to shake up workouts with spinning class, kickboxing, dance, and Pilates. She'll snatch you out of the clutches of eating disorders and into the hands of a therapist/nutrition specialist before they become serious.

4 A VINTAGE-LOVER WHO SHARES HER SECRETS.

We're nostalgia queens. Nothing makes us happier than a rumble through a jumble with a friend who has "a good eye," knows where the best stuff is at flea markets, and how to navigate yard and garage sales.

Thanks to my antique-happy chums, I know a day of "flea-ing" means bring envelopes of real cash, a want list, measurements for furnishings, comfy shoes, and sunblock, or Wellies and a hooded rainproof jacket.

She'll have established relationships with vendors and the right negotiating approach to take with each. Want a Deco dressing table, a crystal chandelier, or antique French garden furniture? A flea-friend knows where to find it cheap. When hunting for housewares, she'll pick you up in her "truck" so small furniture, lamps, and rugs make a quick getaway and delivery to your door. Want to outbid competitors at online sites without overdoing it? She'll cleverly snag that vintage Yves Saint Laurent jacket, Louis Vuitton tote, Fendi baguette bag, or Gucci horse-bit belt for less than you would have and know by instinct when something doesn't feel right. Like maybe it's a fake?!

ONE OF MY BEST GIRLFRIENDS purposely buys white jeans a size smaller on sale in January as incentive to lose extra pounds by May. Know what? She always does!

5 A SOUL MATE WHO'S ON SPEED DIAL.

Everyone needs an alter ego who adores you and vice versa no matter what. She sat through your breast reduction and lift and went new-bra shopping with you after recovery and stayed glued to your side during your divorce explosion and aftermath. She's always got your back.

She's the one you call at 2:00 a.m. to rant about your spouse, cry after a breakup or a cancer diagnosis. Of course, she joins your raving and tears in soothing solidarity.

Your BFF listens to every story—even the ones she's heard a million times, pours you another glass of wine when you clearly need it, and got "twin" tattoos with you to celebrate turning 50 and seal your forever friendship. And she knows when no words are necessary—you communicate telepathically.

6 THE ORACLE WHO KNOWS WHERE TO GO AND WHOM TO SEE.

Forget Internet research, this best-babe has a vast in-depth resource list buried in her brain and is always willing to share. Want a new dentist who uses nitrous oxide, a bra-fitter who understands the big boobs–tiny rib cage dilemma, a mover who won't chip your great-grandma Rose's Quimper dishes, a tattoo artist who can reshape your permanently botched, over-tweezed brows . . . she's your girl.

Set your new leather bag on the restaurant floor and now it's got a big grease stain? She knows the specialist who'll have it looking like new.

Need the name of a low-cost tailor who can reshape your bargain dresses to couture precision? Got it! She's like Siri, just better, faster, smarter.

CAROL E. CAMPBELL

I can count on 1 hand the number of true close friends I have. One I met when I was 2 years old, another I met after college, and the rest I met relatively recently. These are the people I could call in the middle of the night and they would be there for me.

7 THE MATCHMAKER PAL WHO FIXES YOU UP.

If you're single, divorced, widowed, or in a bad marriage, this girlfriend just wants to see you "in a happy relationship." You'll never know how this liaison-lover manages to pull available men out of thin air but her broker skills are "free."

A friend with a wide social circle and the people smarts of a secretary of state can sniff out the good guys from the rejects like a mouse who finds only Brie and Camembert.

One of my great NYC friends from the '80s keeps an ever-changing e-mail/cell list of guys with George Clooney–ish charisma who are newly free or devastated. She manages to dole out the right guy to get their heart off life support. Works like a charm to restore your mojo.

8 THE CULTURED CHUM WHO FEEDS YOUR MIND AND CREATIVITY.

Music, art, reading, gardening, cooking, and blogging are big bonding things for women 50+. If we're not crafting, we're painting, sculpting, planting a vegetable garden, practicing the piano, making pottery, whipping up herbed quinoa with green onions or coq au vin, spewing our daily guts out online, or catching up on the *New York Times Book Review* bestseller list. Bored or boring we are not! And though we can do these things alone, we appreciate the back and forth inspiration of our peers.

A friend who nurtures your enlightened state is a gift to the psyche. She gets tickets for 2 to new museum exhibitions and gallery openings, indie film festivals and concerts, or suggests day trips to historic sites.

BRENDA COFFEE

I never had children so in my 20s and 30s I didn't have a lot in common with many of the women I met. When I was diagnosed with breast cancer that changed. I met the strongest, most amazing women who understood one another and shared the same fears. I really bonded with women then. I started BreastCancerSisterhood.com, a top survivorship resource site for families, after treatment. Many of the women I met then, I'm still in touch with now. At this age we've stopped competing with one another so it allows us to foster a different kind of friendship that's deeper on a lot of levels. My 2 girlfriends since high school are still my best girlfriends.

9 THE GIRLFRIEND WHO MAKES YOU A BETTER PERSON.

She's always been a softie but is tough enough to volunteer for everything from eldercare to animal shelters and domestic violence centers. A caregiver chum who is persistent gives you the push to go outside your comfort zone when you'd never do it alone.

Giving time, energy, and help to others comes right back 'atcha with a renewed sense of well-being. If you're suffering depression or just a bad case of the blues, volunteer work can boost your mood, lower your stress levels, provide a sense of purpose, and create new friendships.

The Peace Corps has a 50+ program in place. You and a friend can even volunteer abroad—working to establish schools, orphanages, etc.

10 A PLAY-PAL WHO INDULGES YOUR SUPERFICIAL SIDE.

At times we all want some R&R, saying "Gimme a break!" from responsibility and stressful life issues. A friend who will indulge your rebellious, youthful, sillier self that lurks deep beneath your grown-up one is needed.

She's the mani/pedi mate who agrees sparkly mermaid blue-green polish is more fun than nude, encourages you to buy glitter ballet flats instead of black leather, goes to chick-flicks meant for twenty-somethings with you—and springs for the jelly beans!

Don't confuse fun with frivolous. This ally is not superficial at all; she might be a financial analyst or CEO of a major corporation. But her soul remembers the girl inside both of you who longs for bikini days at the beach, boys with convertible sports cars, dancing at clubs and the thrill of super-high heels. Depend on her to commemorate major birthdays with a big surprise bash, to plan a girls-only once-a-year trip, and to never laugh at your wish for a big fat cushion-cut diamond ring—even if you buy it yourself!

JEANNINE SHAO COLLINS

I have 5 close girlfriends who know *all*. These I e-mail, text, or talk to every day. I'm making new friends all the time since I love being social but not at the level of "the 5." I usually meet new people through work or my children. As a working mom with 3 kids—Julia, John, and JD—and a fabulous husband of 21 years, my family life is pretty full so my closest friends do understand.

SASS TALK: GOOD FRIENDS CAN TURN TOXIC!

Life is your party and you get to choose the guests! I'm no psychotherapist but women tell me their emotional health and well-being are greatly dependent on quality friendships now.

Real friends always celebrate your wins, mourn your losses, pick you up, or at least prop you up when you fall down. And yes it *is* possible to disengage from old friends you've had forever or people you remain socially connected to in some way . . . I've done it. When to cut the cord? If a friend plays passive-aggressive games, talks about you behind your back, is curt and abrasive one day but sugary-sweet the next, this is not a friend. Move on! And when you do, disconnect with love or at least grace, but guilt-free. No major

> Your friends should always make you feel fabulous, and you never get tired of them.

Your friends should be like the best possible wardrobe basics—they work anytime in any situation, boost your confidence and mood, always make you feel fabulous, and you never get tired of them.

Be picky. Buddies you keep around from habit, history, or guilt emotionally drain your spirit.

discussion necessary. Just be less available and ultimately unavailable ("Sorry but I can't make it" or "I'm super busy right now . . . talk soon"). Speak kindly about her/him/them if the relationship comes up in conversation with mutual friends ("Haven't seen her for a while, but wish her well") and slip away.

JUST BETWEEN US:
10 LIFE BAND-AIDS EVERY FRIEND WANTS

1 A DISTRACTING BOOK.

A great thriller, historical novel, witty memoir, or bio can temporarily kick stress to the curb. I always re-read my favorites and buy extra hard copies (yes, real books!) of don't-miss reads (even those I've read on Kindle) for gifting buddies going through hard times. The Pendergast series by Douglas Preston and Lincoln Child and Jack Reacher books by Lee Child have an empowering kick-ass attitude (even though the main characters are guys), the time-travel *Outlander* series by Diana Gabaldon, and anything Tudor-ish by Philippa Gregory totally remove one from the present, at least temporarily. Memoirs by peers like Anjelica Huston, Diane Keaton, and Brooke Shields have the right combo of gab and sizzle to inspire.

2 ALL YOUR BEST FRIENDS' EMERGENCY NUMBERS.

You should have your close friends' e-mails and numbers (family, spouse, doctor, attorney, etc.) and vice versa. You may be the one present or in charge during a crisis, especially if they're single, divorced, or close family members live far away. Nothing looks more reassuring from a hospital gurney or emergency room chair than a friendly face taking charge.

3 A THANK-YOU STASH.

A real handwritten thank-you note, not a "thx" text or an e-card (though this appears to be trending more and more), is always more heartfelt. Make personal thank-you cards a to-buy. Have personalized notes made, or pick up blank cards with a beautiful photo, painting, or border (museum shops have fabulous ones), or individualize plain note cards with rubber stamps and ink pads. When a friend recommends you for a job interview, fixes you up with her newly divorced plastic surgeon brother, spends days shopping with you for a mother-of-the-bride dress, comes with you to chemo—an immediate grateful word is important.

4 JOKES THAT ARE "BETWEEN US."

Sometimes the one thing that pulls us out of a slump is a giggle. It's never better than when shared with a pal who gets it, too. Certain funny scenes from movies that resonate (for me it's always a Diane Keaton one), a phrase, a reference to an old boyfriend, or a past "gotcha" prank moment can make us roar.

5 A FAVORITE "SPLURGE" PURCHASE YOU SHARE.

This is a riff on the *Sisterhood of the Traveling Pants* theme and works best for truly expensive accessories you seldom wear. My friend Allyn also wears a size 5 shoe and her dressy wildly expensive Manolo Blahnik heels have spent more time on my feet than hers. My friend Ana loaned me a drop-dead Givenchy couture cocktail dress for an industry party and I FedEx-ed it back to her in L.A. She borrowed a vintage kimono from me to wear over a '20s dress for a party on her end.

6 A BUTTON DEACTIVATING STORY.

Historical friends who know one another's life chapter by chapter recall tales and situations from the past that have the power to turn things around. It's the telling of "remember the time" that talks us down off the ledge when we're blue, angry, tired, and stressed out from too many credit card bills, job loss, or a disagreement with our adult kids or husband. My friend Val, who has a memory like Wikipedia, can recall stories from the '60s and '70s that wipe out every bad day in minutes.

MYRNA BLYTH

I could fill my days with lunches, dinners, and coffees but I really have only 2 or 3 very close friends. Still, nobody is the friend my husband, Jeffrey, was. I lost him a year ago and I miss him terribly. He grew up in England and I grew up in a suburb on Long Island, but we were interested in the same things. We were both journalists, knew the same people, and could finish one another's sentences.

7 A RETREAT.

Sometimes we need to vanish, escape, and disappear even if only for a day to think, breathe, come to a decision, or make a plan. Certain public spaces are "islands" of total calm when you're alone, with a trusted chum they're sanctuaries. Museums, libraries, parks, beaches, and places of worship are free (or in the case of museums, low-cost for seniors). The quiet, anonymity, and sense of peace help me organize thoughts for projects, wrestle with problems away from my usual temptations and distractions. I find wandering through big department stores like Barneys and Bergdorf Goodman with earplugs, hat, and sunglasses oddly soothing sometimes—for me it's like taking a cruise . . . but it's not for everybody! When friends need an overnight getaway for whatever reason, volunteer a spare bedroom, a pull-out sofa bed, or a couch and say "make yourself at home, I'm here if you need me."

8 A WHEN-WE-WERE-20 PHOTO.

Or 30 or 40, for that matter. A visual memory of shared moments is a treasure. Recently a BFF sent me photos of us with our now-adult kids at a birthday party. My daughters (whom I consider my friends as well) continue to surprise me by tagging Facebook photos of us when I was a young brunette single mom. I loved revisiting my striped Sonia Rykiel sweaters, denim skirts, Dr. Scholl's, embroidered flared jeans, and Kork-Ease sandals but that tan I had scared the hell out of me to see! If only I didn't barbecue my skin to a crisp at the beach! Still, a flashback from then beats a selfie today!

9 A SECRET CRUSH.

Only your best friend knows you'd sleep with Larry David or Daniel Craig if you got the chance, have a thing for that neighbor who shovels your driveway unasked, that you flirt with your now-married high school boyfriend by e-mail, and wish Leonardo da Vinci would come back from the dead . . . so attractive! It's a harmless infatuation.

[Showing up empty-handed is really not okay. Keep a gift collection handy.]

10 LAST-MINUTE GIFTS.

Maybe it's your BFF's birthday (and you forgot), a chum just got divorced and moved into her own apartment, a buddy finally landed a job again, you're invited for the weekend to a couple-friend's beach house or asked over to watch the Super Bowl or the Oscars together. Showing up empty-handed is really not okay. This is where having extra-special gift items on hand helps. Keep a gift collection handy: a pretty candle, a coffee-table book or new cookbook, a bunch of gourmet lollipops (as a bouquet), a tin of imported tea, a bottle of bath oil or salts, or a sparkly key ring. Just put a bow on it.

BROADMINDED: THERE'S A TIME TO SAY YES, NO, I'M SORRY, AND THAT'S FAAABULOUS!

If any of our friends (including family and neighbors) has a passion or habit . . . say belting out Broadway show tunes while driving, cooking super-garlicky bouillabaisse, growing hideous cacti . . . we encourage, never discourage even if it's not our thing. After all, we don't want anyone disparaging our weird behaviors and inclinations, do we? But a part of friendship is also about knowing when and what to do and how. Here are some suggestions.

LET IT GO.

Learn something from every disagreement. Neutralize shame and regret from old arguments and move on! Replaying the same old tape is truly a waste of time. Don't wreck the present by hanging onto the past.

JUST SAY NO.

When a friend starts spending too much time with a bottle of vodka, has dieted down to an eating disorder, has resumed smoking cigarettes after a 10-year break, is smoking her stepson's pot in the ladies' room at work, or has serious anger-management issues or behavioral problems, it's time to play bad cop. Letting a chum know when her appearance and habits are dangerous to her health is not easy but she will thank you in the end. Expect denial, resistance, maybe even anger, or loss of the relationship. But if you don't have an intervention talk, you're not being a friend.

APOLOGIZE WHEN YOU'RE WRONG.

So maybe that new long-distance boyfriend of your BFF turns out to be a good guy and not a gold digger after all. It's possible you were kind of harsh about a chum's car habits driving to Vermont—I mean is singing the entire new Katy Perry and Adele albums off-tune while crunching veggie chips so bad? Is the way you handled a disagreement or friendly spat truly the only way? Learn how to keep friendships alive even when problems arise by thinking before you speak, taking the edge off difficult conversations with "You may not agree with me but I'm feeling . . ."

BE GENUINELY HAPPY WHEN GOOD THINGS HAPPEN.

Jealousy is a bad friend thing. If your BFF is getting a breast lift and you can't even afford a new bra you're hankering for, or she's taking an 8-day river cruise from Paris to Normandy and you're spending summer vacation break at the town pool, send her good vibes. The boomerang effect will eventually come back at you.

MAKE THE CALL.

Never keep friends in the dark when you're running late. You don't want a friend to sit at a table waiting alone and worrying she got the date/time/place wrong. If you're stuck in traffic, a meeting, stopped for gas, or are looking for a parking spot, let her know.

DON'T BROADCAST DIFFERENCES OR CONFIDENCES.

When someone tells you something in a private conversation and says "this is just between us," it is! Tweeting or outing the news on Facebook is wrong, bitchy, and bad manners. And when a girlfriend says "tell no one," she is including your husband.

SEEK OUT SHY, QUIET PEOPLE.

A lot of incredible people may not feel comfortable in groups. Lure them with a phone call or invitation to lunch. Introverts can have a lot to say if you're willing to be a better listener . . . and a friend. Some women mistake a reserved manner for antisocial behavior—they couldn't be more wrong.

PUT A STOP TO ANNOYING BEHAVIOR.

If you or your chum check your e-mail, Facebook, Twitter, Instagram, or Pinterest constantly while together, stomp your ballet flats and say no more. Same goes for borrowing money for the meter, poaching food off your plate without asking, showing up 20 minutes late every time, or dishing out spoilers to episodes you haven't seen yet. Tell a friend who is always whining, complaining, and criticizing that she needs to put a lid on it. And discourage friends who make snide comments about the children, job prospects, or husband of other friends.

DECIDE IF A KISS, DOUBLE KISS, HUG, OR PAT IS YOUR GREETING.

The meet and greet at a cocktail hour or party, or before dinner is often a dilemma for women 50+. If you do go in for a kiss, start on the right and place your right hand lightly on their left shoulder, lean in so your cheek brushes his/her cheek but not lips. Purse lips but don't make a smacking sound. And if you don't kiss (as several of my low-immune system chums say) just throw them a kiss. A hug is also okay for touchers.

SHARE THE BAD TIMES.

Helping friends deal with aging or sick parents and spouses is a biggie. It's a rite of passage we all will go through—having caring people there, even in a text or e-mail, can be a buffer. Staying close with friends going through a serious illness or divorce and sharing their fears, thoughts, and concerns is also important. Don't stand on ceremony, just get in there and pitch in. Say "what can I do to help?" rather than saying how sorry you feel for them.

KNOW HOW TO DEAL WITH RED WINE STAINS.

Friends who spill red wine on your good table-cloth, rug, sofa, chair, or dress can't quite get it out of their minds and you'll never get it out of yours. Accidental splashes of pinot noir or cabernet sauvignon are inevitable, so here's what you do . . . act quickly! Blot the spill with a clean cloth or paper towels but don't rub or scrub the stain outward. Dab the area with white wine or club soda and keep your blotting technique going. Then pour a ton of salt, baby powder, or baking soda (whatever is available) over the stain. Wait a few hours or overnight before whisking or shaking off the residue. Never bring it up.

DONNA BUNTE

I have good friends from different areas of my life but the ones I see most often are 10 women in my community—we check in, call, or see one another. Then I have around 25 good friends around the world I stay in touch with. Moving to a place where a sense of community is strong changed our lives and we've always traveled as a family, exposing the kids to the different ways people live in diverse parts of the world and feel comfortable with people of all races, cultures, religions, and socioeconomic status. Cooking has become a creative outlet for me and it plays a big role in my friendships and socializing. I love inviting friends over for a meal!

CHAPTER FOUR:

DATING AGAIN?!

LOOKING FOR LOVE
IS A COMPETITIVE SPORT.

Widowed women at our age are nothing new but separated and divorced Boomer-babes certainly *are* and it's a major trend. Late-life breakups are increasingly common. Sometimes you look at your spouse and think "we're really totally incompatible at this point." If you have enough money to live alone, the it's-now-or-never moment becomes more appealing. Most "conscious uncouplings" after 50 are initiated by financially stable women who are still working or have enough money to set out solo. Some women love their new independence and have no desire to couple up soon . . . or ever.

Others head straight into the dating scene. Then we have options. Do we want to try exclusive dating sites for our demo or seniors' speed-dating events, travel tours, marathons, and cruises? Social networking—especially Facebook—makes renewing old friendships and locating old boyfriends easy and painless. But it never hurts to put the word out and let people know you're open to meeting someone new, everyone from your dentist to the dry-cleaner guy hears the latest on that front. Stay active socially and keep it local. Take tennis

CAROL E. CAMPBELL

I do not think anyone should have a fixed idea of who their ideal partner is. You'll be sitting home if you have a whole preset criteria, and people also don't come crashing in your front door. I force myself to make an effort. In fact, I started a game with a few single girlfriends. We agree to go out and each pick one person at the restaurant/museum etc. Then we force ourselves to go talk to them and possibly exchange contact info. You must put yourself in 3+ situations a week where you're not sitting on the sofa in sweatpants. I hate the concept of dating sites and prefer fix-ups by friends, but you have to do it. Refresh your profile constantly so it comes up in searches. I'm not hung up on getting married again but I do want a successful, committed relationship. I would not mind another great piece of jewelry but it does not have to be an engagement/wedding ring. Let's call it a commitment ring.

lessons, volunteer, get involved in community politics, or take a job at a big luxury car dealership (always an amazing place to meet men). And stop being picky about invitations—you get invited to your niece's dance recital, a wine tasting, a wake . . . you go.

AGE IS APPROPRIATE AND AWESOME

Looking for love at 50+ means looking healthy, youthful, fit, sexy (in a not-slutty way), and stylish. That's a start. There's far more to us than the packaging. Our self-assured attitude comes across in body language, voice, looks, and words.

Yes, you could say the online dating game reduces relationships to "shopping," but it expands our selection in terms of sheer volume, possibilities, and personalities.

Our online profile says who we are, what our needs, goals, and desires are today as we seek a smart match. Sure, it's not the "glance across a crowded room" sizzle, but dating sites do connect you quickly to available men and get you going. The reality is some women find online dating exhilarating and sexy, while others find it daunting, scary, invasive, or too much work. The good old DIY approach still appeals to our romantic side, too. We make eye contact with a 40-ish fellow at the gym and ask how to use the elliptical (knowing full well how to, of course), chat up the professorial-looking guy in cords and Converse behind us on the drugstore line, the silver-haired hunk sitting at his laptop in the coffee shop, or the 60-ish Liam Neeson look-alike we nod to while he walks his big Scottish deerhound every evening as we take our own pooch for a stroll. In this chapter, my chums Carol and Alison dish on their dating experiences with lots of smart-ass, saucy advice, too. Take it!

ALISON HOUTTE

I'm a big Match.com fan, after years of denial about shopping for guys online. I work, I sleep, I eat. I'm not going to waste time standing around in a bar trying to get picked up at this point. Online dating is a game and you need to exert total control over who you select to meet. Post your favorite casual photos of yourself (nothing too sexy) and be honest. At 55 I'm seeking guys between 40 and 60. I feel good in that range. The privacy on Match is excellent and I notice men who pay to be on a site are much more serious about their lives. A few tips: No photo or just one photo—pass! Separated—pass! Mentions sex in his profile—pass! His female age range is 25+—pass! Ask all the questions you want and request extra photos but reveal only your first name. Keep it simple until you meet someone deserving of your last name and cell number. Keep it light and don't dump all your crap on them.

LET'S DISH

Don't give away too much too soon. However you meet someone, be honest, but no need to share all until you feel there's enough common ground for a potential relationship. If all you want is someone to see occasionally for dinner or a movie, say so. If you're looking for a long-term commitment, say so. A lot of the women I spoke to date 180 degrees from their past partner . . . at least at first. Makes sense to me! After 40 years with a crabby doctor or tightly wound corporate exec, why not date a free-wheeling pastry chef or a laid-back landscape architect?

Some women come out as gay later in life and choose a female partner this time around (and if that's *you* please don't take my use of "he" personally when I talk about partners or "guys" in this book!). But it's not all about divorce. Widows 50+ decide they're ready for a companion again if not a lover and join the dating scene, too. Don't let age get in the way.

MEANWHILE, GETTING BACK INTO THE SWING OF THINGS REQUIRES SOME STRATEGY:

CHOOSE DATE SITES THAT FIT YOU, NOT YOUR 30-YEAR-OLD DAUGHTER.

Ask friends which sites work best for them. Match.com offers a preview but you won't be able to select and connect until you join up and pay. Search tools help narrow your picks based on interests, age, and location. Other sites, like eHarmony, do the matching for you from a questionnaire. This saves time but plenty of us would rather do the sifting ourselves. How About We has its own site but has also partnered with AARP for an over-50-only selection of peers who suggest dates, from coffee to a bike ride to concerts. It gets you out of the where-and-what-to-do date rut. The planned activity takes the heat off and gives your outing a nice you're-in-control feeling and easy exit strategy.

LEARN TO FLIRT AGAIN.

A real-time first meeting matters. Don't dress provocatively, just appropriate to where you are and what you're doing. Mirror body language to get in sync. If you lean in elbows on the table, he will, too. Mimicking body movements plus using the other person's name draws them in. Touch their arm lightly when making a point to establish light intimacy, too. Meet in a public place, not your home or his! Ask questions, project genuine interest, and react to the other person's conversation. A date is an audition.

KNOW HOW MUCH "BAGGAGE" IS OKAY FOR YOU.

We all drag a past bundle along into our new lives. The question: Is it a steamer trunk, carry-on wheelie, or lightweight duffle? Part of getting to know someone is figuring out what amount of baggage is acceptable and what's a deal breaker. Does he have serious health or money issues? A string of angry exes and bad marriages? A history of infidelity? Different ideas about how to live and where? Is he still putting a kid through school or paying child support? Are his adult kids difficult or problematic? Does he have a cat/dog allergy (especially when you have a Persian cat or an Old English sheepdog)? Think it over.

WEED OUT THE GOOD FROM THE BAD.

It's so easy to edit out men who lack basic communication skills and don't fit our criteria, but how about the walking wounded? Guys who are selfish, narcissistic, angry, emotionally abusive, or bitter often manage to hide their true colors under a veneer of clever words, good looks, a sound career, and excellent storytelling skills. Let your natural protective instincts and humor kick in. Whether you're looking online or are actually on a real-life date, use your intuition and common sense. Don't get distracted by his resemblance to Colin Firth or his supposed access to a private plane and villa in Majorca. Be ruthless. Maybe you're thinking "Is that a hairpiece?" Or "He's had his eyes done!" So *are* these signs of self-absorption or a desire to look younger? If your brain says, "How come he looks different from his photos?" And if those photos include a variety of looks, like a beard, two-day scruff, shaved head, and balding ponytail, let's not mince words. "Spy? In the Witness Protection Program or avoiding arrest?" If he orders the least expensive glass of wine, asks you if your bag is a "real" Hermès or lives with a roommate at 60, no way! Never get involved with someone who will drain your bank account or you suspect is already in a relationship and testing the waters. Be sure he's healthy (mentally and physically) and financially stable. And please remember some men our age prefer the trophy-ism of younger women but date us, too, for real conversation. Avoid those guys!

••••

Q: Why are all my dates duds? Is it me or them?

A: Be adventurous, typecasting is getting in your way.

Sometimes women get so discouraged by their first few experiences they give up. Looking for Mr. Right is not the mission. It's more like being on an archaeological dig or sifting through sale racks. The payoff of dating again is to finally reveal or rediscover feelings and parts of you that have been hidden, buried, or lost for years. Lighten up!

••••

BEEN THERE, DONE THAT

I've spent more years as a single mom, divorced and dating, than being married. Dating as a working mom with a full-time career at any age was not easy; by 50 it was a challenge. When my daughters were young, a revolving army of cheery nannies and quirky *au pairs* provided balance and stability. I was lucky. By the time I hit 50, my daughters had grown to a teen and twenty-something stage and our relationship was more like best girlfriends. We hung out, shopped, traded clothes, and talked about boys, school, and beauty. Men either felt threatened by my kids and lifestyle, attracted to the glamour of my job, or eager to have a dual-paycheck situation with benefits. I never dated online, preferring fix-ups and chance meetings. But since those days Internet dating for the over-50 crowd has boomed. As a writer and beauty/fashion pro, friends ask me all the time to help create, polish, and edit their online profiles and photos. And as a trusted girlfriend, I also get to weigh in on the choices and responses! My advice? Don't limit yourself to one site for the best selection and don't talk about sex or you'll attract every weirdo in your zip code.

LOIS'S TUTORIAL OF TRICKS #4

WE GET IT! 10 CHEATS EVERY DATING BOOMERINA NEEDS TO KNOW

1 PHOTOSHOP YOUR ONLINE PICTURES AND YOUR AGE IF YOU LIKE.

The point of someone meeting you for real is confirmation: yes, she does look like that and the photo is not from 1997. Retouching is not lying, it's enhancing. Think of it like Botox or filler, highlights, colored contact lenses, Spanx, and an underwire contour bra. Go ahead and brighten your skin a bit, smooth out nose-to-mouth creases and lines, erase brown spots, and clean up the whites of your eyes and your teeth. And a word of advice: always be the only person in the photos you post—no parents, kids, exes, or girlfriends.

A little photo deception is fine. In fact, if you don't do it you're kidding yourself because everyone else does.

It's okay to shave a couple of years off the top. Just don't claim to be 48 if you're 56. Hopefully your potential date has the ability to recognize inner beauty and not just appreciate your likeness to Julianne Moore or Goldie Hawn.

> ## A little photo deception is fine.
> ### It's okay to shave a couple of years off the top.

2 BE THE PRODUCER AND SET DIRECTOR OF YOUR SEX LIFE.

Since the liberated '60s, casual sex has gotten a boost from the concept of "hookups" and young celebs leaking sex tapes. And thanks to Viagra and online dating, the rate of sexually transmitted diseases among our 50+ set has rocketed. You need to ask a new likely sexual partner about his health and use condoms—not as we used to for pregnancy concerns but for protection from HIV, chlamydia, and syphilis. Not everyone is "clean" or monogamous, and age certainly offers no resistance to disease. The number of women in their 50s and 60s who have casual date sex is actually small. If and when you do decide to get intimate, make it work for you. Let me share a big sex and body fake-out.

Missionary style—with you on bottom—flattens your belly bulge, makes big boobs look firmer and higher, and hides a saggy derriere, while you on top makes small boobs look bigger and rounds your booty to lushness.

Still worried about extra pounds or flab? Think about those gorgeous, voluptuous nudes by Peter Paul Rubens, Botticelli, and Titian!

3 MAKE YOUR HAIR ADD SEX APPEAL.

Your hair has *one* dating responsibility: to enhance your face and add glamour. Hair is still an important part of physical attraction and while long hair has an alluring reputation, it's not the only solution. We can't all grow manes like Elle Macpherson, Carol Alt, or Demi Moore anymore and besides everyone knows celebs add extensions to keep their big-hair signature looks going. Stylist Chris Cusano of the Brad Johns Color Studio at the Samuel Shriqui Salon in NYC says, "Unless you have thick, healthy hair, don't even waste your time. Really long, thin, stringy, straggly hair makes women look older and unhealthy. Sexy hair benefits from layers, long feathery bangs, and volume, not length."

Your hair can look great unstyled and air-dried (like on an island vacation after a swim or straight out of the shower and to bed) or when fully finished and polished after your styling routine.

It can be any length, short, medium, or long, but it does need to look casual and a little tousled, like you could run your hands through it or get caught in a windstorm and not care. Four basic low-maintenance looks have a grown-up sensuality and a chic attitude.

➤ **A lob** is a longer bob, mid neck to collarbone. Layer the ends or build in texture or waves with product. Lauren Hutton, Katie Couric, and Tory Burch have variations of lobs.

➤ **Long hair** can be blown straight for a classic look, texture-boosted for a wavy, beachy, or trendy bohemian effect. Julianne Moore, Jane Seymour, Andie MacDowell, and Julia Louis-Dreyfus have it.

➤ **A layered, shaggy bob** gets its attitude from long, irregular layers and brow-sweeping bangs. Think Jane Fonda, Diane Keaton, Lisa Rinna, and Helen Mirren here.

➤ **A short, sexy, gamine cut** is sexy on the right woman if you feel comfortable in short hair and have the face for it. Think Jamie Lee Curtis, Kris Jenner, and Ellen Barkin for inspiration.

4 FLIRT WITH EVERYONE.

To stay in the game, exercise your charm muscle every day. This is something French women and men understand from birth.

Have your own inner theme song—mine is Sinatra singing "The Lady Is a Tramp."

Radiate warmth and look people in the eye with delight no matter the age, gender, and situation. Hand out small compliments—a few words about their glasses or dog are always effective. The silent flirt always works on lines at airports, coffee shops, and the gym. Make eye contact, look away, then look back and smile. Men are less intimidated by women dressed down than dressed up—you'll get more conversation strike-ups in jeans than a tailored work outfit. Flirt when you're solo, not with a friend or a kid tagging along.

THE POINT OF DATING or meeting new people is to rethink your life, routine, looks, and relationship for the woman you are now.

5 DON'T MAKE "HAPPILY EVER AFTER" THE GOAL.

We're "in the moment" and getting a husband is not the mission.

The point of dating or meeting new people is to rethink your life, routine, looks, and relationship for the woman you are now.

Some women treat dating like a job hunt and make it a strategic project. Others treat it casually whether they meet people "naturally," browse dating sites, or get set up by people they know. Don't settle. Try on lots of new possibilities. You'll be surprised how much your needs and ideas about a relationship have changed. You also don't need to waste time with someone who is emotionally and physically unavailable . . . as in already married. Lots of married men cheat by going on dating sites out of state!

 VACATION IN PARIS.

Pretending you live in a society that is *not* youth-oriented, like Paris, is a shot in the libido. Even a long weekend will provide a major boost when you've been dumped, disappointed, or depressed.

In Paris, men in their 20s give mature babes the once over as we stride down the street and those looks are respectful but appreciative.

French women also look sexy after 50 and it's no garter belt and corset *Belle du Jour* fantasy. Okay, so not every older French woman is Catherine Deneuve or Carla Bruni. Yet, all manage to make being grown-up a sensual experience 24/7. You can, too—even if you never take off your clothes. Mature women in France just ooze sex appeal and in the least obvious ways—they eat, laugh, dress, gesture, and walk with extra zing. Watch carefully. Copy.

7 EAT! IT'S SENSUAL AND SOCIAL.

You don't have to be a full-on foodie, but men hate dating obvious dieters. It makes them nervous, turned off, and scared by this indication that you might be picky about what you put in your mouth. If you think not eating makes you appear thinner, more feminine, sexier, it doesn't—it just makes you look weird and like you might be difficult about restaurant selections. Just be sure to chew with your mouth closed!

Men like women who can take control—so steak, oysters, sushi, mussels, and bouillabaisse that require a little tact and maneuvering are good.

Salmon and sautéed spinach are great date choices if you actually are watching your weight. They show you eat healthy—lean protein, greens, and omega-3s (just be sure you don't have spinach in your teeth after). And nothing is sexier than licking a smidge of cappuccino foam from your lip. On the other hand, watch what he orders. If he selects vanilla fro-yo rather than salted caramel with a scoop of pistachio, maybe *he's* boring. If he orders anything heavy on the garlic or onions, messy food like barbecue ribs, buffalo wings, or sliders, slurps his soup, and has poor table manners on a date, forget that. Ditch him.

8 IF YOU DATE YOUNGER GUYS, BUT DON'T DRESS LIKE YOU'RE 20.

You are not "robbing the cradle," just experimenting. Look cool but don't try to hide your age. Hipsters, artsy, boho types, tech-y geeks, and the like adore older women with attitude. The idea of all that experience intrigues them and they think we're not as high-maintenance as younger women. Ha! We're (probably) not in any rush for marriage, babies, or moving in together for sure. We know what we're doing in bed and aren't in a hurry to tag a man as a boyfriend.

Stay healthy—smoking, drinking, partying all night is not for us, so don't do it! But do work out—younger men are energetic and it'll keep you from being shy in the bedroom! Jane Birkin, Susan Sarandon, Sharon Stone, and Lindsay Duncan make perfect style templates.

Take college grad classes and work from your iPad or laptop in coffee bars, parks, and museums. Wear youthful brands like Madewell, Zara, Rag & Bone, Agnès B., and Vince in soothing neutrals like cream, sage, navy, or gray. Youngish guys don't wear black as much as we tend to. Add flats, Jack Purcells, or Converse. No mommy-ing him, either. Don't correct his grammar, loan him your car, buy him gifts, or pay for everything. No baby talk or streams of texts and e-mails from date one. One of the problems with younger men is they can be needy.

9 MAKE "MARVELOUSLY MAINTAINED" YOUR MOTTO IF YOU WANT TO DATE RICH.

Look sophisticated if dating CEOs, social media moguls, men with multiple homes, a big bank account, and a generous soul is on your agenda. Make sure the wealth on the outside is only a protective coating for the fortune of emotional depth inside, though!

A devotion to dermatological procedures and head-to-toe grooming are the ground rules. Get to know your local day spa, salon, and nail place—they'll be seeing a lot of you.

Wear classy pumps with shapely feminine dresses and skirts that show your legs! Buy a white coat and wear soft "expensive" neutrals like pale gray, beige, and cream. A woman of substance at 50+ usually has her own money and doesn't think twice about dry-cleaner bills. Discretion is better than heaps of costume jewelry. Stick to pearls, stacks of rings or slim bangles, studs, or diamond hoops.

10 LEARN TO FEEL CONFIDENT NAKED.

Forget about scars— they're battle trophies, not defects.

Ease into being nude with strangers by doing more stripped-down group or public activities: swimming, sweaty Bikram yoga, running in shorts and a tank, getting massages or body treatments at a day spa, or sitting in a sauna.

Forget about scars from old C-sections, appendectomy, and breast reduction or lift—they're battle trophies, not defects.

Make anti-bloat, anti-gas foods and drinks a consistent part of your diet—cucumbers, papaya, bananas, asparagus, ginger, and peppermint tea counteract the gassiness and fullness caused by healthy foods like broccoli and beans. And lay off protein bars that contain excessive sugar alcohols like mannitol, sorbitol, and IMOs (isomalto-oligosaccharides). They can back up your gut for days, making tummy bulge more noticeable!

SASS TALK:
WHO SAYS WE CAN'T BE SEXY WITHOUT HAVING SEX TOO?

It's not just about looks, décolletage, or your bedside manner. After 50, the combo of brains and beauty is crucial. Watch your weight but bulk up your mind with current events, history, politics, whatever's new in books, films, the arts, science, food, and technology. Your everyday conversation and appetite for life is what's really super-sexy.

Plus, keeping your mind alive reduces depression, anxiety, and the urge to blow your IRA on something crazy . . . like new boobs or a trip to Cuba with the guy you met last night. Date a fairly long time before you reveal almost everything—establish a higher level of trust and really get to know someone without feeling pressured into intimacy.

BRENDA COFFEE

I've been married 3 times and haven't had a date in 22 years! Once when a man asked me out I e-mailed my girlfriends and asked "What do I do?" They all came back with "Go!" but I didn't. While I'd like to have someone to go out to dinner with . . . I'm the one with the baggage. I'm scarred from 10 breast cancer surgeries and because I can no longer take estrogen, sex is painful. That's a deal breaker for younger men in my future and I don't want to be some old guy's caretaker.

JUST BETWEEN US: 10 DATING B-BABE MUST-HAVES

Before you begin looking online and rearranging your schedule, check the bait. You won't need all of these, but at least one will make a difference.

1 BELIEF IN YOUR BOOTY AND BODY.

> Shapewear isn't shameful.
> ## It's liberating.

Love your body. One of the super-sexy things about older women is we're not obsessed with being model-thin or perfect. Tushies are *terrific*, so adore yours. I'm not suggesting we wriggle out of our Spanx and support bra—just get more comfortable in your own skin. Shift your mind-set because it's certainly more than okay to have extreme curves as in a bodacious booty, thighs, and boobs—but try to balance that with a small waist and flat tummy.

Most women gain belly fat and lose waist definition after 50 and it bugs us. Shapewear isn't shameful. It's liberating.

When you can stop thinking about your bulges and jiggles, slip into your jeans or that curve-hugging dress and feel like Wonder Woman, you've made it.

2 A REALLY GOOD, MYSTERIOUS PERFUME.

Men *are* sensitive to scents. Avoid one that reminds him of his mother or ex if you can. One ready solution is to choose a brand-new perfume. She won't have worn it! In my experience, most conservative, mature men over 50 can't resist intense white florals and classic scents (regardless of their past) like Chanel No. 5, Joy by Jean Patou, Dior Diorissimo, Quelques Fleurs by Houbigant, and Paris and Fracas by Robert Piguet.

Younger men and creative types of any age are drawn to scents with smoky hints of incense, greens, herbs, spices, and essential oils.

Unusual, edgy scents like Jo Malone Wood Sage & Sea Salt Cologne, Voyage d'Hermès, and Diptyque Philosykos have those qualities. When strangers consistently ask "What perfume are you wearing?" it's a winner. Applying fragrance to a moist base of body cream helps it stick. Apply to pulse points and sweaty spots like wrists, neck, back of knees, cleavage, and let it settle. Resist the urge to rub it in. Your body temperature and skin's own oils and current chemistry (foods you've recently eaten, medications, hormonal changes, and stress) will personalize any scent. That's why you hear women say "I love it on you, not on me" about a scent.

3 AN ADORABLE DOG.

No, I'm not kidding—a dog can be an adoring companion and they're good judges of character. A pet will never let you down, break up with you, text and cancel, develop multiple personality disorder, lose its temper, or accuse you of being self-centered. She'll never care whether you watch Fox News or CNBC. Your furry honey is also a magnet for men; people stop to talk to women who are walking dogs. Hypoallergenic, non- or low-shedding pups like a Yorkie, poodle, havanese, bichon frisé, or a poodle mix win over even "allergic" guys and those who wear a lot of black.

A PET WILL NEVER let you down, break up with you, text and cancel, develop multiple personality disorder, lose its temper, or accuse you of being self-centered.

4 A 5-STAR HOTEL STRATEGY.

If you do get to the sleepover stage, get rid of all your exposed junk—clothes on chairs, old magazines, beauty clutter in the bathroom. Spray the place with a sophisticated, non-girly scent and place diffusers strategically around to keep fresh smells circulating. Jo Malone, Antica Farmacista, Nest, and Archipelago Botanicals make the best. Buy big bunches of fresh supermarket flowers in white—they look more upscale. Iron your bed linens and spray them with your perfume or room spray and turn the covers back like "housekeeping" does. Keep a spare "overnight" kit with a razor, condoms, shaving cream, and a fresh toothbrush. Have a stack of clean towels in the bathroom. And if painful sex troubles you, ask your gyno about newly FDA-approved Osphena, the new non-estrogen daily prescription pill that makes vaginal walls thicker and gives you back your sensuality.

5 DE-BLOAT INSURANCE.

"I feel bloated." We say this all the time due to water retention and shifting hormones. An impending date does nothing to diminish the balloon-like feeling, so here's the trick I learned long ago from supermodels now in their 50s and 60s. Even if you're a shower type, soak for fifteen minutes in a warm tub lavished with two cups of Epsom salts. The minerals dissolve and get absorbed through your skin, draining excess fluid and deflating puffy areas like your tummy and ankles. As a bonus, they also sooth sore muscles and hydrate dry, itchy skin. During the day, nibble on natural diuretic foods like asparagus, cucumber, watermelon, ginger tea, and pineapple to help—no gum, soda, or fizzy water.

6 TABLE LAMPS.

A golden glow head-to-toe warms up your skin and blurs discolorations. Overhead lighting is not your friend! Candles are a nice romantic low-watt touch, but why not stay fireproof with table lamps, gold-lined shades, and soft rosy light bulbs. Dimmer switches offer afterglow insurance. A gradual self-tanner can give your skin a more even texture, just remember to do your back and backs of legs, too! I say always meet for dinner or drinks at a bar or restaurant where you know the lighting is soft and flattering. Depend on Jergens Natural Glow and St. Tropez Gradual Tan Everyday.

7 WILD WOMAN EXTRAS.

Back in the '60s, Bond Girl Ursula Andress wore a leopard coat and boots and Bob Dylan sang about a leopard hat on *Blonde on Blonde*. We never got over it. Leopard and cheetah-like prints are always going to make B-Babes feel sensual, but snakeskin and croc have snuck in as sexy staples, too. Staying true to nature in color is a good idea since neutrals make the print and texture easy mixers. Just wear one of each print at a time with jeans and don't go overboard. Smartest buys: a leopard print silk blouse or pencil skirt, snakeskin pumps, and an embossed croc belt or python bag.

8 A PREPARED "THANKS, BUT NO" RESPONSE.

First dates are unpredictable. Set a short time limit, like coffee. If something feels off (like did someone else write his profile and e-mails?), leave. Say "sorry but I have to be honest, we're not a good fit." You're a grown-up, why would you need more time to linger if he's not right? If it's a second date (let's say dinner or drinks) and you think he's brainless, hightail it to the ladies. Then say you have a personal "emergency" (while waving your cell at him) and leave . . . alone.

Buy BLACK LACY BRAS and matching girl shorts. Suddenly you're a pinup, not a porn star. This is the new world of dating underwear . . .

9 A BREAK-UP BOOSTER.

Tipper Gore and Maria Shriver bounced back from splits looking better, happier, and more delighted than ever. It's the ultimate satisfaction. If someone you've been dating calls it quits, do something ASAP to get gutsy and gorgeous again. Join a gym or yoga class. Then buy a luxurious "go-to-hell" buttery black leather something—like trench coat or boots. Go out—a lot. This is where your girlfriends do backup. Stock up on kohl pencils and mascara. Crisp but smoky lined eyes can vamp up your mood in 5 minutes flat.

10 SLIPS IN BLACK LACE.

We buy sexy lingerie for our own comfort and confidence mostly. Remember Elizabeth Taylor in *Cat on a Hot Tin Roof* or even Anne Bancroft in *The Graduate*? A full slip is like wearing a little sexy dress that clings. It can be minimalist sleek, lacy, or even have built-in shaping power. Make it black. It shows more shape than flesh and won't look the slightest bit tarty. Throw one on to brush your teeth or make coffee. A little secrecy is always sexier than revealing all. Buy black lacy bras and matching girl shorts. Suddenly you're a pinup, not a porn star. This is the new world of dating underwear and nude or white seamless microfiber just won't do.

BROADMINDED:
PREPARATION IS EVERYTHING!

Do not do a makeover on your boyfriend or potential spouse no matter how overweight/poorly dressed/combed-over he is. Think *Beauty and the Beast* with you as Beauty. Otherwise he will follow your makeover suggestions—slim down, get fit, shave his head or get a transplant, learn to self-tan, start buying cool glasses and hipster clothes at J. Crew instead of Dick's Sporting Goods, and trade in his sedan for a sports car . . . and start dating 30 year olds. As a happily married lady I can now reveal date-land was time-consuming and expensive. I always had an extra bottle of Veuve Clicquot on hand, fresh French cheeses, pâte and figs in the fridge, rice crackers, and olives ready to be warmed in olive oil. At all times my home smelled like Diptyque Baies candles, with comfy throws everywhere you looked, artwork from my photographer chums, bookcases lining the walls and a stack of wood next to the fireplace . . . in other words boyfriend-ready. Here are my best personal dating 50+ tips:

NO OBVIOUS VANITY.

Blatant narcissism is not sexy. Having the self-assurance to not fuss, fidget, tug, or perfect our looks on a date is far more attractive than checking yourself out in the mirror or adjusting your clothes. What's the worst that can happen? Your liner will smudge? Even sexier. Your layers will get a little askew. Even more stylish. If someone pays you a compliment, smile and say "thank you."

SMOOTH FEET AND A PEDICURE ARE ESSENTIAL.

Feet with soles of tough dead skin and crusty toe cuticles are not sexy. So go ahead and get a salon paraffin treatment and reflexology and a fierce toe polish, but don't leave it at that. Daily softening cream with shea butter and botanical oils or an exfoliating salicylic and glycolic acid cream work wonders for upkeep.

GET A SLOUGHING ROUTINE GOING.

Dry, dull skin means war. As we age, our natural cell-renewal process slows to a crawl. Dead cells sit idly on the surface of the skin, blocking oils, creams, lotions, and even self-tanners from working effectively. You need two things: a facial exfoliation duo in the form of gentle creamy cleanser paired with a sonic exfoliating brush like the Clarisonic Mia. Then add a shower or bath scrub to slough off "body dandruff," the cells that flake off inside black tees and leggings. De-fuzz at home, too. You don't need a salon Brazilian or bedazzled va-jay-jay at 50—just trim things up. Big surprise: after menopause, our pubic hair gets thinner so it's not such a chore. Then slather on your oils and body creams to restore a plump, firm dewy look to freshened skin.

MANAGE YOUR MITTS.

No talons or squared-off shovels! Only two nail lengths and shapes work for us: a short, rounded square, which looks workable, modern, chic, and youthful or a medium-length almond shape that makes short, stubby hands look leaner and younger (but make them no longer than ¼-inch past your fingertips). Darker colors are now classic and wearable at any age. For a natural look, choose the right nudes: tanned hands look good in whites and beige-y nudes while mature hands with blue-based undertones, blue veins, or a red-weathered look benefit from subtle pinky-nudes, especially those with a slight shimmery finish, which makes nails sparkly and glossy for an illusion of radiance and health.

SAY YES TO LAST-MINUTE DATES.

No more "he'll have to call me by Tuesday to see me Friday or Saturday." Instant dates are cool now that technology and fast living make planning obsolete. So if he e-mails, texts, or calls to meet for a coffee or glass of wine and there's no time for a shower or even a quick trip home . . . don't stand on ceremony. But what if you're feeling "fat," dirty, and tired? Here are 5 quick tricks to pull off a transformation.

➤ **Add face glow.** Grab an ice cube and sweep it over your face and lids to wake up your skin, right over any makeup you're wearing. Blot, then dab your cheeks with tinted lip balm or lipstick before doing your lips.

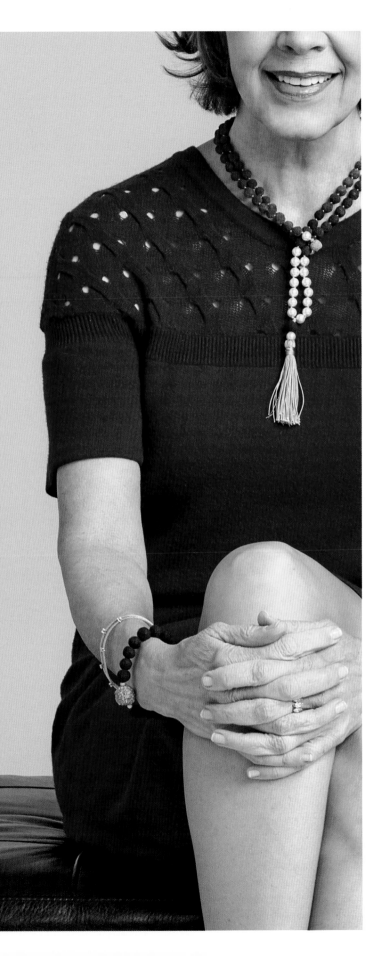

Show some skin. Roll or push up your sleeves (even blazers and coats look less serious when you do this). Roll your jeans at the ankles. Unbutton your shirt to a V just above your bra and cleavage.

Tousle your hair. Bend at the waist and run your fingers through your hair and flip it back. Switch the part to the opposite side or do a zigzag one for lift.

Get back some dewiness. Check your bag, desk, and tote. If you have some hand cream, moisturizer, a tube of Aquaphor, eye cream, sunscreen, a vitamin E capsule, or a sample foil of face cream—mix a dab in your palms first. Tap some on your cheekbones, cuticles, ends of hair and brows, too.

Add scent. This is why you should carry purse spray or a rollerball scent. Failing that search magazines for ads with scent strips. Stroke the scent over wrists, throat, and nape.

PACK SELECTIVELY FOR A SEXY WEEKEND AWAY.

Take only a few items you love and always include a tailored jacket and a trench coat, a dress *or* a skirt. Wear your favorite jeans, that blazer, a relaxed tee or sweater, flats, and your daily jewelry (any rings, pendant, or necklaces you never take off). Works whether you're staying at a B&B, a hotel in the city, or his cabin in the country. Bring heels, flats booties, and a couple of print tops and scarves to vary the basics.

KNOW HOW TO GO TO A BAR ALONE.

Try a low-key place rather than a glitzy one with a dressed-to-kill clientele or a crowded pickup place. Stake your spot—at an end of the bar to drink, nibble, eat, and people-watch, or smack in the middle to be social. Make friends with the bartender or a cocktail waitress who can help if some crackpot is hitting on you orcan call you a cab.

SOMETIMES, BUT NOT TOO OFTEN ... ACT LIKE A GUY.

Men—especially ones under 50—do say they like when women drink whiskey or beer instead of white wine or a dirty martini, come straight from yoga or a run all sweaty in a tank and yoga pants, watch a game on TV and scream at an appropriate moment, laugh and talk dirty during sex. As I said, not too often.

DEAL UPFRONT WITH "GHOST" DATERS.

Online dating has unfortunately created a disposable dating culture where guys think it's okay to text and call us obsessively and then vanish. Sometimes a guy you've been seeing slowly fades away with no discussion. Take charge with a "wish you well but we're clearly not a good fit" e-mail or text so you don't feel dumped or duped.

AUDREY SMALTZ

You have to stay open to the unexpected. I married my best friend, Gail Marquis, who was a basketball Olympian in 2011. I wasn't thinking about dating but once we met we never shut up, and marrying a *woman* was a surprise, but it's the best thing to ever happen to me. We absolutely complement one another and have expanded both our lives.

CHAPTER FIVE

THE GLAM-MA THING

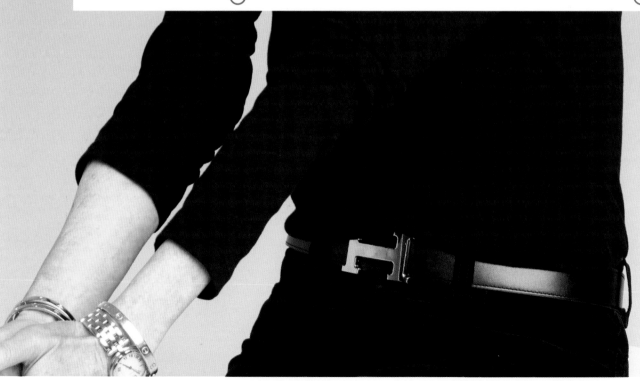

GRANDMAS 50+ WITH SIZZLE ARE WEARING TIGHT JEANS AND DOING YOGA.

The word "grandma" is not always easy. "Mom" at least still has a youthful zing! So we opt for alternative titles like GG, G-ma, Mom-mom, Mimi, Mimsy, or Mumsy instead. Sharon Osbourne goes by "Shazza" while Blythe Danner's grandkids call her "Lalo." Goldie Hawn and I do "Glam-ma." Old attitudes about being a grandma have been deleted by glamorous poster girls who glorify granny-hood. Let's call them—and ourselves—Glam-mas, because we are. In addition to those mentioned, add Tina Knowles, Carole Middleton, Jane Seymour, Kris Jenner, Chaka Khan, Jessica Lange, Rita Wilson, Catherine Deneuve, Laura Bush, Diane von Furstenberg, Sarah Palin, Sally Field, Ivana Trump, Emmylou Harris, Nancy Pelosi, Gloria Estefan, Gladys Knight, Reba McEntire, Kate Capshaw, Susan Sarandon, Jane Fonda, Martha Stewart, Priscilla Presley, and Suzanne Somers. We make the combo of age, style, and grandkids appealing.

AGE IS APPROPRIATE AND AWESOME

We're way more flexible and effective nurturers as Glam-mas than we were as moms and are certainly more easygoing than those micro-managing kids of ours. We're more relaxed about homework, the "I-don't-feel-good" thing on test days, sibling spats, and not wanting to eat vegetables (okay, we'll just sneak them in smoothies and disguise them

We think daydreaming, free play, and just hanging out with an old-fashioned real book, bike, guitar, or dog are healthy and encourage creativity. Clearly a full-time circus of childcare helpers, including day care, nannies, babysitters, and other grandmas is no substitution for a fabulous Glam-ma. This is an odd twist. We who started the

> Our grandkids instinctively know we are a refuge from parental "enemies"

as juice!). We're indulgent, funny, filled with interesting facts, and couldn't care less about rules . . . unless we make them.

Our grandkids instinctively know we are a refuge from parental "enemies" who text, call, monitor, and over-schedule their every minute.

"me" generation are simply smitten with our grandkids. This does not mean we're obsessed with them. We like our freedom and independence too much for that. We can pick and choose how much time to spend together and where. Two weeks of summer vacation together at our house or a day at the beach? An afternoon playdate at the park or a weekend sleepover? A daily chat or once-a-week call? So listen, talk, pile on love and attention, help when and where you're needed, and then do your thing. This, too, is still called "balance."

MYRNA BLYTH

I have 2 grandchildren, Katherine and David, 1 from each of my 2 adult sons. Katherine is like a mini version of myself—interested in everything I do, conversational, loves beauty and fashion. We have a blast. David is divine, affectionate, sociable, funny, and a joy to be around. But I'm not an "OMG!" kind of grandmother who can't wait to hear from my grandkids. I commute between New York and Washington so I don't get to babysit, but I am thrilled to be a grandmother . . . or Glam-ma.

LET'S DISH

Grannies with glamour combine new energy and ideas with old-time soothing skills. We've learned to love kale and quinoa, matcha tea, and probiotic yogurt, but ask us to whip up comfort foods like lasagna, blueberry pancakes, or chili any time. Spinning, yoga, or Pilates are on our to-do list, but kid-time to walk in the park or swim keeps our muscles and bones happy, too. Encouraging our grandkids to exercise by example makes even our couch-potato *adult* kids feel guilty. We like to move and briskly. Some Glam-mas don't just drive . . . we zip around on a bike, Vespa, Harley, or in a Jeep (with a car seat or 2 in back).

Since we are the original counterculture activists, trust us to know sleepovers are for staying up late, watching *Frozen* for the fifteenth time, and eating chips and ice cream. Of course, we're clearly capable of sticking to the healthy snacks of apple slices with peanut butter, carrot and celery sticks with hummus, and strawberries with yogurt that their mothers suggest . . . although we're guilty as charged more often than not.

HERE'S WHY THEY NEED US MORE THAN EVER NOW:

GLAM-MA-ING IS HEALTHY AND MUTUALLY BENEFICIAL.

Multi-marriages are increasingly common, so often we're one of a few grandmas in a complex family. Increased social engagement is one of the big perks. We get a chance to expand our network of close relationships, be part of a bigger Mothership, and make new connections that can improve our social and work lives.

These days it's not unusual for older Glam-mas to live-in as part of an extended household or stand-in for working daughters and daughters-in-law as a full-time "second" mom. Glam-mas who go this latter route get to combine finances with their kids and all benefit from intergenerational wisdom. This keeps us young, belonging, and feeling loved and that's always a healthy boost. As Glam-mas separate and divorce, the idea of adding on a housing unit to an existing home or renovating a garage apartment does come up. Built-in babysitters are always in demand . . . but on our terms, please.

IT'S NOT ABOUT BEING A MINI-ME ANYMORE.

Grandmas used to peer into their grandkids faces for proud signs of self-recognition—my nose, auburn hair, dimples, or green eyes. But now grandkids often don't look like us at all. With adoptions soaring, sperm or egg donors commonplace, our own kids marrying people with kids from previous relationships, that's becoming the rule rather than the exception. Add biological grandkids who look like the other side, step-grandkids, foster grandkids, and anything goes. It's all about raising healthy kids and making sure they have a good education, values (kindness, honesty, confidence, a positive attitude toward life and others), and a desire to achieve. We make sure that happens.

EDIT NEWS, TEACH COMPASSION.

The news is pretty terrifying for kids today. They see plane crashes, earthquakes, mass shootings, wars on TV, and hear about them at school. For Glam-mas it's distressing and for kids it's *really* upsetting. Younger kids can't handle discussions or photos of disasters and may be frightened by what older kids say on the bus or playground.

We have plenty to shield them from in everyday life, like drug and alcohol abuse, death of a family member, divorce and our own health issues, let alone worldwide carnage. Turn off the news until they're asleep or catch up online. Kids do suffer from depression and anxiety. Let them know they're safe. Share positive stories with them from the news—developments in space, science, technology, and human-interest stories. Teach them to have compassion for kids they see at school and around town who have health challenges that set them apart—those in wheelchairs, kids who are autistic, or have speech problems and physical or learning disabilities. It's a life lesson they won't forget.

....

Q: Why are friends who are not yet grandmas
snarky when I show photos?

A: It's called j-e-a-l-o-u-s-y!
Ask to see a photo of their recent vacation
or home renovation.

You can't prepare for Glam-ma-hood no matter how supportive and involved you are in the 9-month (or less in the case of adoptions and marriages) prep work. It's not anything like being a mother. You move to another level of parenting that is simultaneously freeing and strangely expensive. Who knew babies and little kids now need so much stuff or that the luxury market would go after the wee kid set with such ferocity. The boost is due to older parents who are financially set and competitive and celeb parents making branded kid stuff the new normal.

The cribs, bedding, prams, high chairs, and diaper bags alone could bankrupt a Glam-ma who doesn't watch her checkbook. Baby and kid everything have created a new level of crazy expensive items—from top-of-the-line strollers for $1,400 *and up* with special liners, carrying case attachments, canopies! There are coveted diaper bags by Gucci and Stella McCartney, pricey Moncler and Duvetica puffers and snowsuits, kid Uggs, and Hunter rain boots. And the competition for whose grandkid has what is wild! Makes me nostalgic for the days when my own baby girls were happy with what were *then* low-cost Petite Bateau tees, OshKosh overalls, Keds, little print floral dresses from cheapo giant Prisunic in Paris, and their simple Umbroller strollers…so was I.

....

BEEN THERE, DONE THAT

True confession. I am not a perfect conventional grandmother but then again I wasn't a perfect daughter or mother, either. But I am on the upside of good and my daughter and grandsons don't seem to notice my lack of constant involvement in their everyday lives. I'm a Glam-ma in my grandsons' pack. There are also 2 grandmas, 2 stepgrannies, and 1 great grandmother (my mom, GG), who may be the coolest Great-Glam-ma of all. I'm not the most hands-on of the bunch but maybe that's because I never had male offspring and my grandsons live for sports. I'm a total loser at soccer, football, baseball, golf, skiing, and basketball, though my not-so-frequent babysitting gigs include marathon sports sessions of Xbox. However, my grandsons do call me once or twice a week, write to me from sleepaway camp over the summer, know I will not reveal secrets, and count on me to smuggle in those chips and chocolate, and buy them the T-shirts they want instead of the ones their mother suggests.

Sometimes I think I blew it as a single mom, often putting my job and social life before my daughters, so I work harder now as a mom and grandma to be patient and listen more, not break promises, be there and be "present."

Just ask my daughters. Their don't-tell-her-anything-till-she-takes-you-shopping strategy was formed in retaliation for my lack of availability. In the end, what makes my daughters happy as adults today is pretty much the same thing that would have made them happy at 7 or 14. We love hanging out together.

SOMETIMES I THINK I BLEW IT
as a single mom, so I work harder
now as a mom and grandma.

LOIS'S TUTORIAL OF TRICKS #5

WE GET IT! 10 THINGS GLAM-MAS STILL LOVE, TOO

1 ANYTHING TO DO WITH DINOSAURS, WHALES, OR OUTER SPACE.

Some things never change. Take us to New York's American Museum of Natural History along with its Hayden Planetarium Space Show and we're in heaven. Almost literally. That combo of historical awe and extraterrestrial wonder has stuck with us since we were kids ourselves. Watch *E.T.* with your grandkids to spark their curiosity about the universe. We're probably not going to sign on for a Virgin Galactic trip but what B-Babe and kid over 7 hasn't wondered about the possibility of intelligent life elsewhere in the universe and UFO sightings? No need to visit an observatory with hi-tech telescopes—an at-home one or binoculars make great birthday presents for your young stargazers. Buy them books and beginner science kits (the Discovery Channel has fantastic ones!) to stimulate hobbies.

By reading up on prehistoric dinosaurs, the planets, or gemstones together you may be encouraging future paleontologists, astronomers, and scientists and stimulating your own brain cells to stay active, too.

Who can resist a whale-watch boat ride? Guided by marine biologists and naturalists, they're available along the U.S. coastline, including California, Hawaii, New York, Cape Cod, and Alaska. Depending on the location and time of year you can spot different types like gray or blue whales, orcas, and dolphins, too. Bring your camera, iPhone, sunblock, and anti-nausea meds or ginger candy if you or the kids are prone to seasickness.

2 THEME FESTIVALS AND FAIRS.

There's an almost nonstop schedule of events all over the country that serve multiple purposes. They dazzle grandkids and expose them to new ideas and spur better mental functioning for us.

Choose ones that appeal to you both or just you guilt-free since you're exposing them to a world far removed from the hassles of everyday life, nonstop news bulletins, and routines.

If you're inspired, the day may lead to your own involvement to "work" these fairs. Give anything from Renaissance fairs (complete with historical costumes, food, and entertainment) to rodeos, folk music festivals, flower shows, country farm events, and arts and crafts fairs a try.

3 FUNNY MOVIES.

Laughing together is fun and healthy because it helps relieve stress and depression for Glam-mas and kids. Here's why: laughter promotes the release of endorphins (those feel-good hormones that exercise also boosts) in the brain, which relaxes muscles and lowers blood levels of the stress-out hormone cortisol. Kids today have to deal with bullying, ramped-up school pressure, family issues (divorces, childcare situations they dislike), and a range of psychological and physical disorders that make life tough. Our ability to lighten up can free them from feeling cornered and vice versa.

You may have to learn to love animated characters and get used to new superheroes, but giggles are contagious and ageless.

Grab the Skinny Pop! Favorites which include *The Croods, ParaNorman, The Avengers, Finding Nemo, The Incredibles, Shrek, Muppets Most Wanted,* and *Alexander and the Terrible, Horrible, No Good, Very Bad Day.*

4 KID-FRIENDLY FARMS WITH ANIMALS TO PET AND FRUIT TO PICK.

I always feel like a Mrs. Drysdale straight out of *The Beverly Hillbillies* sitcom on a farm but that doesn't stop me. Younger grandkids are always fascinated to find that eggs, milk, and apples aren't "born" in their local supermarket. It's a nice low-stress intro to healthy nutrition for picky kids and those with eating disorders or sensory issues.

A farm visit is a reminder for us to eat a healthy, balanced diet and to stay "alkaline" with veggies and fruits as we age.

Dermatologist Dr. Jeannette Graf says "diet plays a huge role in having firm, clear, healthy skin after 50 and veering toward alkaline foods like spinach, broccoli, kale, avocados, blueberries, and green tea is the way to go." Seeing how fresh food is grown and processed, picking your own plums, peaches, apples, or strawberries could flip your diet sensibility and theirs. Check local farms for visitor dates and activities. Some have petting zoos where grandkids (and you) can pat rabbits, pigs, and sheep, bottle-feed baby goats, take a tractor ride or hayride (especially around Halloween), and have a picnic.

5 PLAY OLD-FASHIONED "THINKING GAMES."

Our thumbs are numb from e-mails and texting. How about we try checkers, cards, chess, Scrabble, or a jigsaw puzzle?

Playtime that doesn't require batteries or an electrical outlet, gives us a needed dose of nostalgia, and boots us back to our own childhood.

I'm not suggesting bingo, mah-jongg, or poker—just age-free vintage games that could be a quiet-time activity for them and trigger new brain cell formation for us while reducing our cognitive decline. And when it comes to outside play, whatever happened to tag, hopscotch, jacks, or jumping rope? I kind of miss them—you, too?

6 CREATE A GARDEN WITH A LITTLE "HELP."

So you never had a green thumb until now. A love of nature can be encouraged in kids from an early age just by growing your own organic veggies, herbs, and flowers. My friend Marilyn started her own vegetable garden based on one she saw at Versailles and her granddaughters, Katie and Claire, painted and labeled large smooth stones to indicate what goes where in a rainbow of hues. A clever creative way to keep track of what's growing. Gardening keeps our senses alive and teaches kids about the environment and weather in a hands-on way.

The more senses you use, the better your memory, and gardening uses all—sight, touch, taste, hearing, and smell. Scent is the most powerful of all in boosting our memory bank.

Kids benefit from establishing a sense of responsibility, too. After all, someone has to water and care for a garden, weed it, and prevent pests from destroying all! Even toddlers can be encouraged to dig in the dirt and plant seeds (just be sure they're old enough not to eat either one). Older kids can help make a scarecrow. Take them to visit community gardens for ideas.

7 PUBLIC PARKS WITH TRAILS FOR WALKING, CYCLING, AND SITTING ON A BENCH.

Kids love park playgrounds, but get them to walk with you by making it a project. Bring the dog (reason to rescue one from a shelter ASAP) or get them a pedometer, too, and start tracking steps each day. Taking 10,000 steps is suggested for maintaining health, between 12,000 to 15,000 for weight-loss. Need more aerobic fitness? Increase the speed and brisk walk for 3,000 of your steps. The real reward is an adequate workout for Glam-ma but throw in a frozen yogurt as a finale and bring along bottles of water. Dehydration is not acceptable. Honestly, my favorite playground thing to do is sit on a swing and swing. It makes me feel around 7 again, if only for a half hour.

8 THE BEACH... WITH SUNSCREEN.

Of course, Glam-mas are world-class sandcastle builders and shell collectors, but we also like dips in the pool and ocean. My daughter Jennifer and grandsons Ryan and Ian are respectively horrified and grossed out when Glam-ma Lo (me) shows up at the pool in a bikini. I'm told grandmas baring private bits (like a little too much boob or tush) is still not okay, except if you live in Malibu or on a French island. Yes, Goldie Hawn, Kris Jenner, and Carole Middleton have sexed up granny-hood but our national aging-body paranoia makes beach etiquette not negotiable for Glam-mas. Here's how to not let anyone scare you into a muumuu.

➤ **Blur away brown spots, loose dangly bits, and other signs of age** that are apparently too "public" for family affairs with self-tanner. By bumping up your base skin tone, age spots, broken capillaries, and veins are less obvious and flabby arms and jiggly thighs look somewhat smoother and firmer, too. For speed, this product delivers an immediate sweat-proof sunny glow as your faux tan develops.

➤ **Do a one-shoulder swimsuit.** Instead of showing your boobs (another no-no) try a one-shoulder one-piece swimsuit. It turns on your inner goddess with a toga vibe, showcases fabulous shoulders (and *all* Glam-mas of every size have them) but covers your cleavage. Choose any color or print you love. You can bend over, take a dip in the pool, hunt for shells at the shore, or dig a moat without breast bounce or spillage. It doesn't look vampy like plunging V necks or halters.

➤ **Select details that help achieve the best you.** Suits that are shirred, draped, or have built-in compression panels manage a mushy middle or bloated tummy with ease.

➤ **A high-cut legline is mandatory.** It adds inches to your legs on top, which, in turn, trims your thighs, and creates the illusion of longer legs. It's this base that makes your body look great on the beach. Think of a long stem on a full-blooming flower.

➤ **Add accessories with glamour.** Slip on charismatic big dark sunglasses, a straw hat with a peek-a-boo brim, and add a jet-set stylish floaty tunic or airy lightweight caftan when the sun gets to be too much or you want some coverage. No sloppy sarongs, chunky oversize tees, or baseball caps for Glam-ma. Skip skirted suits (dowdy and who are you kidding?!) and straight across "retro" styles (super fattening, leg shortening, and frumpy) and stop worrying about "full-rear coverage." Puh-leeeze, a smidge of tush cheek is adorable and not in the least offensive on us. Go ahead. Ask any man.

9 A FAMILY VACATION TO A FOREIGN COUNTRY.

This gives you, Glam-ma, a chance to use that new language you've been learning and to challenge your brain cells (again!) with maps, planners, and apps for places of historic interest. Taking grandkids abroad—whether it's to a big city like Barcelona, Prague, or Tokyo, or islands like the Bahamas or Turks and Caicos—is an opportunity for them to experience new customs, people, history, foods, cultures, and scenery. My grandsons are big on swimming and skiing and anything to do with snow, beaches, river rafting, volcanoes, snorkeling, and dolphins gets their interest, so the super-cultural, anthropological, historical places will just have to wait.

10 HOLIDAYS.

Glam-mas usually get into the whole Halloween, Christmas, Hanukkah, Kwanzaa, Fourth of July thing. Anything with a hint of glitter, festive accessories, parties, and a reason to break out the fun fashion part of our closet has that effect. I'm not exactly Glam-ma Poppins but I can get motivated. First there are all the possible outings—day trips to special museum exhibitions or concerts, plays and musicals, barbecues, family brunches and dinners, holiday movies, indoor and outdoor ice-skating rinks, sledding, or malls crammed with kid-themed events. Then there's all the at-home stuff: we dance around to holiday music, get crafty with clay, paint, or cook tiny savory hors d'oeuvres for friends and family.

SASS TALK: NEW FAMILY COMBOS NEED NEW SOLUTIONS!

Things are not what they used to be. For example, here's how a Glam-ma Thanksgiving works in my family now. My older daughter, Jen, (and her husband, Marc, and my grandkids) goes to her dad's family (he was husband #1); my younger daughter, Alex, either goes with Jen or to a friend's family; my mom and sister, Rebecca, spend the meal with Beck's husband's family; my brother, Steve, and his kids feast with his wife's family; my husband's adult kids spend a vegan-vegetarian Thanksgiving with their mother; and my husband and I get dolled-up and go happily out to a restaurant.

However, there are times when Jen (who has a Martha Stewart–like gene from who knows where) ignores all divides and invites everyone from all families to parties and barbecues throughout the year so we feel connected. Then she sends major photo albums (hundreds of pics) online to all. Don't get caught up in creating a contest for best grandma or expect a gold trophy. It's not *always* about you. Tradition is great but evolution is inevitable, so stay fluid.

JUST BETWEEN US: 10 THINGS EVERY GLAM-MA NEEDS

Glam-ma is a new word that defies a strict definition. It's not about money, being wrinkle-free, or wobbling in stilettos and designer togs after your grandbabies while an entourage of nannies and personal assistants snap the moment for Instagram. A Glam-ma can be 65, live in a one-bedroom apartment in a tiny suburban town, drive a vintage VW Beetle, spend her days on a laptop in jeans and ballet flats; or she can be 52, live in a McMansion, drive a brand-new Lexus, have a high-powered career, and dress like a supermodel. What do we all have in common? Charisma, a certain sense of beauty and style, razzle-dazzle and allure that one never used to associate with the word grandmother. Never mind what celebs do on camera, *we* all need:

1 COMFY SHOES.

Glam-mas need shoes that really let us dash around, drive, walk, run (if we need to), and combine style and practical thinking. We collect fashionable loafers, driving shoes, moccasins, ballet flats, and flat-soled boots at every opportunity for that reason. And, of course, because flats are less likely to result in hairline fractures or osteoarthritis from possible ankle injuries, too. Heels remain part of Glam-ma-ism for work and dressy occasions and because we can't totally bear to give them up. But by now we understand that tapered toe pumps with lower heels can do the leg-lengthening job 5-inch stilettos do and give our bony feet a break.

Add slip-on sneakers, clogs, and contoured sole sandals with soft adjustable straps that are now officially fashionable to your stockpile, too.

2 HAND SANITIZER, ANTIBACTERIAL WIPES, AND A GERM-SMART ATTITUDE.

How germ-phobic should Glam-mas be? We change diaper poo and wipe tushes, clean up vomit, blow noses into tissues, prepare their snacks and sometimes meals, give them baths, take them to the pediatrician, and supervise playdates sometimes. So without being neurotic, how can we avoid germs, bacteria, and worse, staph or E.coli? Most dermatologists I interviewed suggest using hand sanitizer when you can't wash your hands and you should—a lot. They say also wipe off your cell and stop touching your face so much!

But the menu at the neighborhood diner—where the kids love to go with Glam-ma to—is germ central. Bet you never thought of that one!

As Dr. Day says, "You can't get crazy. Hand sanitizers are useful (but drying) and the one overlooked filthiest place to consider are restaurant menus, which are loaded with germs and bacteria—unless they're the paper kind that get replaced daily." Cold and flu viruses can last on hard surfaces for 18 hours, so in a busy restaurant hundreds of people are passing germs onto you via the menu—so get out the sanitizer after ordering. Same goes for grocery cart handles and magazines in doctors' waiting rooms. At home, color code your towels especially during winter cold and flu season and don't keep your sonic toothbrush on the counter next to the toilet (which you always flush with the lid down, right?). Then just swab down high-touch spots like computer keyboards, pens, faucets, handles, doorknobs, arm rests at theaters, and on planes with antibacterial wipes but don't make it an obsessive-compulsive thing. We don't want grandkids picking up on that!

3 BLACK LEATHER.

Basics aren't what they used to be and neither are grandmas. When a black leather motorcycle jacket is the equivalent of a navy blue blazer, blue nail polish is as normal as red, leggings are considered pants, and even ladylike pumps are covered with studs, Glam-mas have options. The secret is to stay fashionable but not look desperate or overdo the trendiness to the border of tackiness.

Here's what we can count on to give even the most low-key lifestyle an edgy twist: add a black leather classic anything.

A tailored and well-cut black leather item like a knee-length pencil skirt, lean jeans, or a lady-like cropped jacket (if a moto jacket is not your thing) give every lifestyle wardrobe from urban to suburban an edgy pop. Glam-mas with a diva-like personality and a more advanced fashion taste will, of course, be tempted by a leather dress or peplum top for work. Choose soft, buttery real leather or faux which is now considered an A-list alternative, not a poor substitute for the real deal at all.

4 A LOW-COST WRINKLE CREAM THAT REALLY WORKS.

Smart Glam-mas know a good moisturizer, like the right lipstick, doesn't have to be expensive. It just has to do the job perfectly. People see our face, not the package the skin cream came in. A cream that hydrates dry skin, plumps up lines and wrinkles, fades and prevents brown spots, and brightens depends on proven ingredients. Good multitaskers are RoC Retinol Correxion Deep Wrinkle Cream or RoC Multi Correxion 5 in 1 Daily Moisturizer. Look for one or more of these on the label or package:

➤ **Retinol and peptides** reduce fine lines and wrinkles.

➤ **Essential oils** improve radiance and dryness.

➤ **Glycolic acid (an AHA) and salicylic acid (BHA)** accelerate cell renewal for smoother, fresher skin.

➤ **Hyaluronic acid and glycerin** are humectants that attract water to plump up lined skin.

➤ **Antioxidants and niacinamide** prevent and fade brown spots.

5 A WEATHERPROOF WARDROBE.

A little bit of allure never hurts when sloshing through puddles and snowdrifts, sledding with the kids, sitting on the floor, digging in the garden or sand, walking the dog, going down the slide, finger painting, or watching a hockey match. Every Glam-ma needs clothes that look good as they perform. We need:

➤ **A waterproof—or at least water-resistant—hooded parka** (the hood offers extra and instant hair protection whether you wear a hat or not);

➤ **Slim puffer vest** to wear solo over a tee or sweater or layer under a coat or raincoat.

➤ **Slim ankle pants, non-jean leggings, or cropped jeans with stretch** to wear with . . .

➤ **Rubber rain boots** (so you can splash in puddles, too!).

➤ **Warm, fleecy snow boots with lug soles** that grip in rainy, slippery weather.

➤ **Soft relaxed tees, hoodies, and slouchy sweaters**—a stack of them.

6 A VAGUE WORKING KNOWLEDGE OF SPORTS.

You don't have to actually play or totally understand the game (as I've learned), just get familiar with the overall scheme, rules, and teams. For example, know that baseball has nine innings, football and basketball have four quarters, and soccer has two halves. They'll fill in the important details. For school or camp games, pitch in, supply snacks, bring binoculars, and take pictures. Going to grandkid games you don't want to cheer at the wrong time or for the wrong team (as I have) or the wrong kid!

AUDREY SMALTZ

I do a lot of mentoring to my young Ground Crew staff but I also have a stepdaughter and 2 grandchildren—a 17-year-old grandson and a 15-year-old granddaughter whom I'm so proud of! Every stylish Glam-ma needs to spend enough time on staying active and healthy and then work the clothes. You need your best-fitting jeans, a great black dress, a perfect raincoat—mine is red, capes for drama like my 2 black cashmere ones trimmed in fox and leather fringe, the right bra (and please get it fitted properly), Spanx shapewear, a swimsuit you love, and pants that fit perfectly.

7 SEXY DRESS-UP EXTRAS.

Every Glam-ma in the public eye from Camilla, Duchess of Cornwall, to Jane Fonda counts on sparkle and bling. Whether you're going out for the evening or to a family celebration show your shape, cover your cleavage, and add some glitz. Slim pants in black sequins with a black cashmere sweater or a nipped waist tuxedo jacket over a white silk blouse with jeans or a black leather pencil skirt looks elegant. Always have: jewel-studded belts, statement bib necklaces, sparkly or metallic clutch bags, and a dressy topper like a black satin trench.

8 A SMILEY FACE SOMETHING TO REMIND YOU TO GRIN.

Know what? Mom was right. For some of us, our face did freeze that way! And it makes Glam-mas look grumpy. You know those smiley face T-shirts and emoticons that force a cheery face? They have the right idea. Smile as much as possible because over a lifetime, habitually frowning, wrinkling your forehead, and scrunching up your face may have drilled those grooves in place for good. Stick with your tooth-whitening (procedures or at home strips) so even permanently down-turned lips seem sweeter and wear fresh lip colors, like pinks and roses that look healthy and upbeat. And get a smiley face fridge magnet or keychain!

9 A NO-TECH DAY OR WEEKEND.

Of course, we and our grandkids are Internet savvy, but that doesn't mean we have to live it all the time. Ban the cells, don't check e-mails, sales alerts, or Facebook, and spend electronic-free, off-the-grid time. For us, going retro for a day clears our brains, allows us to solve problems, and really spend time being more aware, more in the moment, and takes us off autopilot.

You'll be surprised after a no-tech break how many items in your online site "shopping bags" get downgraded to "wish list" or deleted once the pressure to buy from e-mail alert reminders is gone.

When it comes to grandkids, try instituting a no video-gaming, no-texting couple of hours with them, too, where conversation and discussions are not filtered through the competition of tech devices. For older grandkids, this is the time to have one-on-one talks about things they can't or won't discuss with their parents—periods, tanning, backne, hook-ups, friends who smoke pot, crushes, piercings, and their problem of the day.

10 SUNSCREEN EVERY DAY.

Glam-mas know skipping sunscreen is the path to wrinkles, brown spots, and skin cancer. So they choose the right sunscreen ingredients, like: avobenzone, homosalate, octisalate, octocrylene, oxybenzone, Helioplex technology, Mexoryl SX, zinc oxide, and titanium dioxide. And we shmear our grandkids, too! Even the best skincare regimen can't prevent further damage without the use of broad spectrum SPF 30 sunscreen 365 days a year. Be sure to include your neck (especially the sides) chest, backs of hands, and legs if you're going barelegged. The sun is not selective and many melanomas in women are found on the legs.

UVA/UVB rays have no weather filter, so don't use cloudy, hazy, rainy, or cold days as an excuse to slack off. UV rays penetrate all the time and UVA rays (the long-term, skin damaging ones) nab you no matter what the temperature or weather!

Apply sunscreen to drive to work or when working in front of a window indoors because UVA rays do penetrate glass. No more sitting at an outdoor cafe on vacation and thinking a little unprotected natural vitamin D is okay. It's not. Buy drugstore sunscreen, not luxury label brands. You're going to be using a lot of it, so get practical. Write the opening date with a Sharpie on every sunscreen you buy since oxygen degrades the SPF. Toss leftovers after a year.

BROADMINDED:
MAKE "ME" TIME A PRIORITY, BUT BE THERE FOR THEM, TOO!

Being a Glam-ma doesn't mean you're available anytime, anywhere, on demand. You owe it to yourself to stay in shape physically, mentally, and emotionally. Sign up for Zumba, read your Kindle, shop for shoes, spend an hour on Facebook, see a film, take a sculpting or ceramic class, meet friends for lunch, walk on the beach, and leave your guilt behind. When you do visit, you don't have to talk about the baby for 5 hours, clean the kitchen, or do the laundry. But you do have a role to play that moms can't or don't do today . . . teaching your grandkids to be the kind of people you'd want to hang out with at any age. They really do listen when we say: please eat your veggies, use a knife and fork not fingers, wash your hands after using the restroom, use a tissue, and (later on) please use condoms for disease prevention, always feel proud of who you are and stand up for yourself, and I will always be here for you whatever your problem of the minute is. Here are some other Glam-ma-knows-best tips:

BE THE PERMISSIVE ONE.

Glam-mas are allowed to be impractical, sneaky, and even naughty. We buy complicated dresses (read non machine-washable). We can't resist kid sneakers with sequins or glitter, tiered tees with tulle borders, cashmere onesies for newborns to poop in, wildly expensive video games, sports equipment, and designer jeans by Ralph Lauren that will be too small in 5 months. We get the longed-for puppy or kitten birthday gift and retro toys like checkers and crayons in giant boxes of 250.

TEACH BY EXAMPLE.

Have friends of both sexes and all ages around. Bring in takeout meals with new-for-them foods and taste everything with them. Insist on etiquette but laugh your head off, too. Defuse arguments and tantrums with hugs. Be a nouveau tech wiz, but teach them chess and take them to art galleries. Know who's singing on the Top-40 station but turn on jazz, too. Wear fitted clothes that show curves (granddaughters pay attention to body pride) and never fat-shame, age-shame, or gender-shame anyone.

TELL THEM YOUR EXPECTATIONS STRAIGHT ON.

We like to think they'll continue to pay attention when we say: don't *ever* smoke or *ever* do drugs (although we're pretty sure they'll try pot and alcohol somewhere along the way between high school and college), don't curse—it's vulgar, stop adding "y' know" or "like" every few words, never bully anyone or treat them differently regardless of race, religion, size, shape, looks, or gender—we're all equal, and never trash-talk or kiss-and-tell. I try to teach my grandsons to cook, draw, flirt nicely, treat women with respect, and embrace their own quirks and imperfections.

CATER HOLIDAY MEALS.

Why not give yourself a break? Time to relax and enjoy great food and family without labor-intensive, time-sucking chores. Make Thanksgiving, Christmas, New Year's, the Super Bowl, Fourth of July, and big birthdays easy by having pros do the work. Make simple takeout look "homemade" by swapping foils and plastic for your own dishes. Add a few fresh unexpected ingredients to ready-made salads, like quinoa, edamame, salsa, thinly sliced fennel, lentils, or avocado. Sprinkle easy desserts like ice cream with coconut flakes, pretzel bits, and caramel, popcorn, or peanut sauce.

HAVE A PRIVATE ADVENTURE.

Try ecotourism if you're green-focused and go bird-watching, see waterfalls, hike, make a vacation include a new sport like cycling or skiing, or just take a food-and-wine based cruise and indulge for once. And know that Glam-mas who want a major life swivel can always join the Peace Corps or work overseas as teachers. And, of course, dating counts as adventure, too.

CHAPTER SIX:

STYLE HAS NO
SIZE OR AGE

BECAUSE REAL LIFE IS NOT A PHOTO SHOOT.

We live in an era when being thin and looking youthful are a universal goal. The pressure to be slim is why we've been dieting and counting calories for the last (how many?) decades. How much space we take up, what size we wear, and whether or not we should be wearing a body-fitted dress or tight jeans *at this size and age* seems to be everybody else's business. And know what? People actually say so sometimes. At its extreme we call this behavior fat-shaming. But there are exceptions. Apparently if you're famous enough and have a big personality (and enough money) being a woman of size, age, and substance is okay.

As we get older and either get cosmetic surgery or choose not to do so, that topic, too, becomes a matter of public opinion. Women 50+ who clearly have had a face-lift or look suspiciously good and *may* have had a face-lift get talked about. If you're famous the "work" is then critiqued to death in the media. If you opt out and wear your wrinkles like royalty, you either get age-shamed for it or applauded, depending again on how famous, rich, or well-dressed you are. Fat- and age-shaming

KAREN OLIVER

I've made total peace with my body. I never have and never will color my hair or go down the injectables road. I've been sewing since I was a young girl and find joy in making and designing my own clothes. I always have my eye out for something unique that fits my style. It's about high-low dressing for me. "Labels" are not the deciding factor when I'm making a selection. I love to find amazing one-of-a-kind finds that can punch up an outfit that is basically simple. My two biggest beauty secrets: #1 smile and #2 always take the high road and stay positive.

often go together after 50 and they simply *have* to stop. But it's up to each of us. Do you feel guilty hovering over the 50 percent fat free ice cream in the freezer aisle instead of the fresh beets and kale? Do you prefer winter to summer simply because you can hide in loose layers of black every day? Do you look at a svelte woman in a movie theater clutching a wastebasket-size tub of buttered popcorn and think "How could she?!" Well, don't.

AGE IS APPROPRIATE AND AWESOME

Confidence in our looks should be instinctive now, but so should wanting to look good. It simply helps in every area of life. The danger is getting sucked into the whirlpool of cosmetic surgery and diet and taking it to an extreme level. Right out of the starting gate we're a diverse group who have our individual opinions on these topics.

Take 11 women 50+, as I did in this book, and they will all differ in terms of looks, size, body shape, style, and how they deal with age.

What counts is the desire to be healthy and fit and enjoy the way your body in its right-now state acts, looks, and feels—even if it's a work in progress. When we look in the mirror and see our eyes sparkle, our smile grinning back and know there's a clever, witty, playful woman out-smarting age behind them. We all manage our own way.

So let's stop comparing our current body and face to the one we had at 25, 35, or 45. Then let's stop comparing ourselves to other women our age, including celebs.

It's a start and helps put things in perspective. You don't desperately *need* a plastic surgeon, gym membership, cleanse, tummy tuck, or gastric bypass surgery, although if you choose to that's fine, too. But do it by choice, not intimidation. We can't have a gang mentality about age and be judgmental. Here's a more down-to-earth goal: keep your weight steady. The best *you* is the real you in its healthiest state, whatever size you wear. And girlfriends, FYI "average" size is now a 14.

RENE SYLER

I've never been a real fashionista. I love nice things like everyone else; it's just that I tend toward comfort and frugality, no matter the size of my pants or paycheck. I just feel better in comfy bargain finds rather than fussy things that cost a lot of money. When asked to try out for *The View*, in typical Rene fashion I went out the night before in search of a fabulous frock—raced in, found it, paid about $120 before heading off to Target for a belt for $4 and wore shoes from my closet. That's the story behind the polka-dot dress I'm wearing in this book. I find dressing as I get older a bit tricky. I want to be current but I don't want to dress in a way that looks like I'm trying too hard to recapture my youth.

LET'S DISH

Let's assume you're not getting paid big bucks to be a spokesperson for a diet brand or chain of workout centers, or the "face" of a major beauty brand. In that case the only critic that counts is you. I *am* concerned about those of us in denial—women who continue to do crazy harmful things like tan "for real" in the sun or use a sun-bed at a tanning salon and smoke e-cigarettes smugly feeling they've kicked the nicotine habit. I am worried about those who don't exercise at all and totally disregard the quantity and quality of what they eat. We all struggle with ageism. Don't make it harder on yourself.

WE ALL FEEL LIKE:

A YOUNG SOUL TRAPPED IN AN OLDER BODY.

That's why we bring photos of Kate Moss or Amy Adams to our colorist, haul magazine pages of Keira Knightley in Chanel ads to the makeup counter, look at Michelle Williams in a Louis Vuitton ad and think "I can look like that!" Oh yeah? That's your brain, heart, and soul, honey, not reality. The truth is we're all a little more like Dame Helen Mirren in her fabulous L'Oréal Paris commercial. Offered a seat at a bus stop by a young woman she smiles thank you and glowers knowingly at the camera, goes home, applies her L'Oréal Paris Age Perfect moisturizer, changes into vampy red lingerie, and a black leather motorcycle jacket, and goes for a walk, where she glances with intent at a young guy stretching before a run. Game on! Be inspired, but be realistic.

WE SHOULD STOP COMPETING WITH OUR PEERS.

Do you really think women with deep pockets, a face-lift, a big job title, a hot husband, or a size 0 wardrobe are truly more content than you? Probably not. I know plenty of women who fit the description above and *they* worry nonstop. And honestly, even married, smiley-faced, successful, sculpted, and taut celebs, TV stars, and CEOs (and their everyday real women counterparts) over 50 have contentious breakups and divorces, buy the wrong clothes, diet to an unhealthy level, get stressed and depressed, and go to bankruptcy court.

WE SHOULD APPRECIATE THE PERKS OF MENOPAUSE.

Menopause needs a personality makeover. Instead of focusing on its negative reputation, be happy post-menopause. B-Babes like us can wear white jeans and never again worry about period stains. We can have sex without birth control. We can enjoy a migraine-less life since once our hormone turbulence settles these annoying headaches often disappear. We even pee less frequently as the fibroids pressing on our bladder shrink. And best of all, we get a renewed rush of energy. Why not think of menopause not as a drag but as a spark, like charging our cell phone and use that power surge?

Q: Are "boyfriend" jeans "mom" jeans in disguise?
A: Only if you're a mom and forget to roll the cuffs, cinch the waist, and add sexy shoes!

We're not giving up on jeans as three of the women in this book clearly demonstrate. The "boyfriend" style popped in 2008, when Katie Holmes appeared in slouchy rolled ones with ballet flats. We saw an alternative comfy jean that wasn't stuffy or "mumsy" and decided to borrow it for ourselves. Now all you have to do is replace "Do I look fat in these?" with "Do I feel great in these?" or even better "Do these make me look fabulous?" I'm going for that!

BEEN THERE, DONE THAT

My face, body, genes, and style are pals. Don't hate me because I'm thin. I've always been a lightweight shrimp. Small in stature and small-boned, I'm simply genetically hardwired for slimness. Like my vibrant parents, I never thought much about weight or wrinkles. I figured out my own 90-minute at-home mash-up of ballet and yoga early on and have followed it daily since 1965, adding free weights in 1997 and long daily walks with my Yorkie Poo, Louie. My diet has been my own consistent concoction, too: salmon or some other fish (even sardines and anchovies), eggs, turkey, spinach, quinoa, yogurt, veggie burgers, raw nuts and seeds, berries and pineapple, ginger, and lots of tea and water. Would a nutritionist sanction it? Probably not but it works for me. Over the last 10 years,

of course, I do see changes. There are deeper expression lines and crinkles around my eyes and my lids are crepey. My thin lips and baby fine hair are thinner than ever and, though my weight is the same, my body has shifted things around a bit. But I do believe personal style has no age or size—so my jeans, black leather Belstaff motorcycle jacket, T-shirts, bikinis, and boots aren't going anywhere.

And FYI I do follow the advice I give you. I'm determined to keep my body strong and flexible, if not perfect (as my Spanx collection will confirm), my hair healthy, if not lush (and blonded up like a 100-watt light bulb), and my skin juicy and glowing if not firm (I have sun damage, sorry, Mom, I should have listened). Wrinkles and age don't scare me, skin cancer does.

LOIS'S TUTORIAL OF TRICKS #6

WE GET IT! 10 AGE AND BODY TRUTHS

Every woman takes at least 2 sizes of anything into the dressing room because … you never know. We like options and have imagination. And we know sizing is erratic. We always order dressing on the side knowing we'll have it all anyway—just in drips and drabs. The control makes us feel better. We cringe at the date on our driver's license and passport but have no problem getting senior discounts, especially at the movies! Some people would say we're in denial. I say we live in hope.

1 MOST WOMEN DODGE THE AGE ISSUE UNTIL 65.

It's admirable to come out and tell people how old you are and some women proudly do. I don't know many. Most women I know who have had rejuvenating cosmetic surgery or dermatological procedures done and are anywhere from age 54 to 65 say they are 52. Funny but true—all suddenly 52. Those who have had no surgery, fillers, or Botox say "I never discuss age." Sixty is apparently taboo, too, until you turn 65, and then you go around raving about Medicare and your AARP supplemental insurance coverage and drug plan like you discovered gold in your backyard.

When you tell friends "You look great!" please don't add "for your age." It demeans them as well as you.

NANCY GANZ STEIR

I'm proud to tell my age and always have been. Feeling sexy at 60 has its challenges. Exercising and staying fit, eating healthy, and going out having fun really makes a difference in how my face looks. I rarely diet but there are times I watch my carbs, portions, the late-night eating, and step up my exercise routine (spin classes and running on the treadmill). I don't see any harm in a little Botox, filler, or laser for brown spots. I had my eyes done about 10 years ago more because of heavy lids than anything else and had veneers done on my teeth to cover tetracycline. I was always a size 8 with a bit of a belly but after my risk-reducing bilateral mastectomy my belly fat was moved to my breasts and now if I gain a few pounds the weight goes there!

2 IT TAKES A VILLAGE TO LOOK *THAT* GOOD.

Don't be envious of older celebs and supermodels. First of all, they wake up looking as disheveled and tired as we do. They've told me so in interviews. What's really inspiring is their diversity in looks and attitude toward aging. And, of course, even with great hair and makeup, and designer clothes, art directors still can't resist a little Photoshop. Airbrush specialists take away lines, wrinkles, and bulges and add hair or longer legs to provide a flawless image.

In person, up close, most 50+ celebs are clearly older women who look impeccably groomed, beautifully dressed, perfectly made up, and glamorous . . . not young!

That's the big initial shock. Some are truly beautiful with incredible genes; others just have good bones and distinctive features or are a carefully crafted combo of cosmetic dermatology and surgery on top of a nice face. But in each case it's the entire package that makes the real difference. It's the voice, personality, smile, body language, posture, personal style, and self-assurance that transform average-looking women into extraordinary. Don't envy celebs 50+, thank them. They're helping erase ageism for all of us!

ALISON HOUTTE

I love sharing my age and to me imperfection is perfection! We have a history! Why remove the life out of your face? My life salad is a little of this and a little of that but all the ingredients bring balance, nourishment, flavor, passion, and longevity. I need tennis and Pilates twice a week, expensive moisturizer, 6 glasses of water every day, Swedish fish twice daily, 8 hours of sleep a night, a mani/pedi every other week, long layered hair and bangs, a smoky eye makeup, a good bottle of perfume, a little dark chocolate, yummy prosecco, frequent phone chats with my 4 sisters, and an hour-long massage every 2 weeks. I'm all for white teeth, hiding the gray, nice nails, a great bronzing powder, a healthy diet, and a fresh Maybelline mascara.

3 OWN YOUR SIZE, WHATEVER IT IS.

Gaining and losing weight is a common issue for plenty of women. It's why we hang onto "fat" and "skinny" clothes . . . just in case. A backup rack of clothes isn't doing your psyche any good. Get over it! Besides, we need the closet space.

Whatever your size now is the real you. Enjoy it and stop looking over your shoulder.

Every woman has a size in her head that she "should" be as opposed to the truth. It's as true for jeans as bra size and shoes. And while we're dis-cussing size flipping, let me share my own purge. A recent bra fitting revealed I'm now a genuine 32C, not a 34B, prompting an edit in that depart-ment. Sorry to see some of my favorite beauties go but if they're not doing the job, they're useless. My extra low-rise French jeans size 24 (I'm now a 25 or 26 depending on the brand) got trashed along with my too-short pile of tees . . . my body and belly doesn't want them around anymore.

> Whatever your size now is the real you.
> Enjoy it and stop looking over your shoulder.

MAURY ROGOFF

I ponder about sleeping in Spanx only to wake with that fit, shaped, shapely body. In my 20s I needed lipstick to go out on the street, now I need a quick go at the eyebrows, mascara, and lip-stick to get me out the door. As for "outside beauty assistance," there's Frank. Frank Friscioni at Oscar Blandi, a true scientist (aka colorist) has made my tresses blonde and blonder with high-lights and balayage. About a year ago, feeling nostalgic and armed with a photo of my brunette self cradling my then 1-year-old son, I asked Frank to send me back to my original color. He did. I hated him. So for 3 weeks I was miserable, invisible, and both my hair and mood were dark. As soon as Frank deemed it safe, I had my head in foils again. I'm a blonde to the core forever.

4 YOUR NECK IS GORGEOUS.

You can hide it, fix it, or brazen it out, but give your face and body a break. Whatever you don't like about them at 50 is just replacing something you didn't like at 20, 30, or 40. Who decided a crepey neck at 55 is any worse than back fat at 25? For me, a wrinkled delicate neck is like a vintage pleated Fortuny dress or a priceless piece of 18th-century lace, not what some women call a "turkey gobbler." And just add a neck and chest cream to your routine! RoC Multi Correxion 5 in 1 Chest, Neck, and Face Cream keeps you dewy hairline to bra-line.

Who made the call that deep-set, hooded lids at 60 are any worse than puffy peepers at 30? To me they're bedroom eyes that hint at nights past and tales to tell . . . not age. Have you ever seen the *Mona Lisa*!

Who says loose arms and not-taut tummies should be covered at 60 but untoned flabby ones at 28 are fine? To me, soft buttery arms and little pillow bellies remind me of Rubens, Titian, and Botticelli. In the 16th and 17th centuries, any women 50+ with generous curves, fleshy bodies would be hotties! Get yourself to a major art museum and lose your inhibitions.

5 EXPECT YOUR WEIGHT TO VARY.

You're not imagining it. Every female body fluctuates from puberty to way after menopause in weight and size—we go up and down a few pounds and it's all absolutely normal. Your body has not skipped out on you if it keeps changing its mind. Think of the "weight number" in your brain like a basic outfit. Extra pounds get layered on or off. When life gets rockier than usual the constant changes and transitions impact our hormones and habits—including sleeping, eating, and exercising. A few pounds up and down are life.

Expect some weight "waviness" when you're under stress, working more than usual, traveling, preparing for a major life change or challenge like divorce, moving house, or kids leaving home.

Here's what helps your body and brain deal best: a balanced diet. No need for extreme measures when you need to lose 5 or feel super bloated, puffy, and tired. Work on reducing (if not eliminating!) sugar, caffeine, alcohol, fat, salt, and sodas and add more water, fruit, veggies, whole grains, and fresh water fish.

6 GET OVER YOUR EYEBROWS.

What happens when your brows are suddenly the one thing between you and looking good? Bangs! Ask any of us left with skinny commas, tadpole shapes, or half brows. Of course, a hormonal imbalance or a thyroid condition may be responsible for missing brow tails, so get tested if this is your issue.

After 50 even full brows lose hairs. First try growing in your brows for 3 full months and use makeup to shape.

Don't remove any hairs—even those you think are not really part of your brows. Re-growing the front end of over-plucked brows is tricky and slow. Do not be tempted to pluck "strays." Start using brow makeup to compensate. The more you practice, the more authentic your brows will look. Unhook and correct the comma-shape by straightening the line of your brows with tweezers and makeup. Removing the hairs from the front curved underside and then filling in is the only way to stretch and elongate your brows. Patience! Your brows may appear thinner at first but they'll have a more youthful, elongated shape.

7 FACIAL HAIR IS NOT DOING YOU ANY FAVORS.

Unfortunately, after menopause peach fuzz above your upper lip may have darkened or turned into whiskers. This detracts from our dazzling smile, newly whitened teeth, and seems unfair. New hair here when we're losing it on our heads and brows? Our diminished estrogen has left us in the lurch once again and hormonal changes are the culprit. Old options like plucking, bleaching, waxing, threading, using a depilatory, shaving (gulp!), or the prescription cream Vaniqa, which slows hair growth, are all temporary solutions.

A hair removal laser treats light hairs and darker skin tones; it's pricey but permanent.

Dr. Paul Jarrod Frank, founder and director of the 5th Avenue Dermatology Surgery and Laser Center, says "the newest, fastest most painless way to deal with this surge in dark lip hair is the Light-Sheer Desire Laser that can permanently remove hairs in 4 to 6 treatments—each taking 10 minutes or less." Well, this *is* a big improvement over previous hair removal lasers that require at least 10 treatments in 45 minute sessions. Worth it!

8 YOU NEED "CORRECTIVE" HAIR PRODUCTS NOW.

Everything about our hair has changed. It's now one or more of these: thinner, drier, more chemically processed, coarser, graying, fragile, porous, or damaged from heat-styling. Yet we stick to a routine and products like we're 25. Why? It's time to try:

➤ **Upgrading and downsizing your blow-dryer** to a mini travel-size ionic one with multiple heat and power settings and a cool shot button to reduce frizz and frying. They're lighter, and easier to maneuver than full-size ones.

➤ **Leave-in styling oils, elixirs, and spray serums** for scalp *and* hair to encourage repair, growth, strength, mending of split ends, and shine.

➤ **Protein-infused treatments** that protect hair from heat-styling and fill gaps in weak, breakage-prone hair.

➤ **Overnight and in-shower moisturizing hair masks** that transform very dry, damaged hair without making it feel heavy, greasy, or tacky.

➤ **Non-detergent, low-suds hydrating shampoos and conditioners** that baby weak hair.

➤ **Vitamins and supplements** like Aviva and Viviscal Extra Strength Hair Growth Supplements and biotin (aka vitamin B7) do help encourage new growth and repair to garden-variety thin, mature hair.

DONNA BUNTE

I'm 56 and really don't mind my wrinkles. They're lines of experience. I think I'm relatively lucky genetically but I can gain weight. If I start to I do a healthy cleanse, eliminate things from my diet, and make sure I exercise regularly. I like acupuncture for facial rejuvenation. You're not drastically changing your face—just stimulating muscles to tighten, increasing circulation and collagen production, and getting rid of stress (which can change the way we look and feel). Each woman has to make her own decisions about age and how far to go to improve her looks. I think there's a lot of media pressure to be young and women go too far. I always thought I'd have a long gray braid and lots of wrinkles. That may still happen! For now I dye my hair—I'm not so sure about the long gray anymore! I still feel sexy but in a different way. When I'm fit, energetic, well rested, and well nourished, my body and energy reflect that. For me that's sexy.

9 CHOOSE GLASSES LIKE THEY'RE PART OF YOUR FACE.

Because they are. Frames sitting smack on your nose become a new facial feature. Don't get trapped by frames that work on your best friend or a model in a magazine. Their face size, shape, features, and facial details are not the same as yours. Some guidelines:

Shape comes first. Bold black or tortoise frames are #1 go-tos for definition and impact. Pop them on and any woman 50+ looks cooler, hipper, smarter, younger, sexier! Aside from helping us see, they provide style benefits that go beyond trend appeal.

Simple, strong, frames with a "geeky" or "bookish" look are classy and edgy at the same time and in a medium size have the fashion staying power of classic black pumps, a tan trench coat, or LBD.

➤ **Angular frames with strong edges** and squared lines work like tailored clothes to reinforce structure. This shape is Wayfarer-inspired and great for mature faces that have lost a firm texture, round faces, and those of us who show weight gain in our cheeks and chin.

➤ **Frames with rounded edges** or rounded bottoms add definition to our eyes but also soften the effects of a deep nasolabial fold or downturned lips. When it comes to sunglasses, the butterfly shape that swoops and arcs or even the classic teardrop shape aviator style does this job.

➤ **Frames with a subtle upward tilt** work like an eye lift for saggy eyes and brows. The updated cat-eye frames in modified sizes and shapes are sexy and glamorous.

Face and feature size influence eyeglass size. In general, bigger frames work best for B-Babes with a firm jaw and high cheekbones, a full face that's rounded out with weight gain, or a big personality that can carry off attention-getting glasses. Scaled-down versions of dramatic or trendy styles work for smaller, thinner faces and delicate features. Bold, thick frames and more refined frames in identical shapes offer the same face-flattering benefits and style, so you're not losing anything by editing proportions.

Shop online for frames, but pre-shop by trying frames in actual optician shops or "reader" departments to nail the shape, size, and look. Whether you're looking for ready-made readers, sunglasses, or Rx glasses, the extra detective work is worth it. Try affordable sites like warbyparker.com, framesdirect.com, coastal.com, and eyebobs.com.

10 LET YOUR "QUIRKS" BECOME SIGNATURES.

Stop trying to erase
the character out of your looks

Something happens after 50. The small individual "flaws" that have bugged us for decades become trademarks and we start to appreciate them. They're the things that make you, you.

Suddenly that gap between your front teeth, wildly curly hair, the white streak you've had in your brunette locks since turning 20, your prominent aquiline nose, or lopsided smile turn into attributes.

Stop trying to erase the character out of your looks by correcting the very things that give you individuality!

SASS TALK:
WHO SAYS WRINKLES, GRAY HAIR, AND A FEW EXTRA POUNDS AREN'T SENSUAL?

We've eased up and taken a few tips from younger women who consider what we used to call flaws, assets! They embrace and even exaggerate curves with tight clingy clothes, booty-boosting panties, and the tightest jeans possible. Big boobs are celebrated with gorgeous super-strength bras fancied up with lace (FYI, the new average American bra size is a generous 34DD). They consider muscular legs sexy and wear booties with short skirts to show them off. Instead of thinking "makeover," go with what you've got. Better start loving your curves. I defy you to look at Catherine Deneuve, Suzanne Somers, Marcia Gay Harden, Viola Davis, Oprah Winfrey, or the robust and riveting Judy Dench and say otherwise.

JEANNINE SHAO COLLINS

I'm 50 and I don't mind saying so. Working in the glam publishing industry with beauty clients, how can I *not* be interested in everything and anything that'll make me look and feel great? There is certain pressure to keep up—Botox, fillers, Fraxel, designer clothes. I don't like my brown spots and it's hard for me to lose weight, but overall I'm very comfortable in my own skin. I spend a lot of time in restaurants and that makes dieting difficult. I have to cut out sugar to lose weight; it's not *all* about working out. Lipstick makes me feel great, too. It's my big beauty thing but I'm lazy about eye makeup. I always wear lip color—anything from a berry stain to bold red.

JUST BETWEEN US: 10 THINGS THAT GET BETTER WITH AGE

And now for the stuff we don't focus on but actually improve our looks and sense of well-being. How about that vintage black leather motorcycle jacket that makes us feel like Katey Sagal in *Sons of Anarchy*, or the wooden mirror frames we gilded one rainy weekend and now have that peeling, antique-y look we love, and those pickles in the back of the fridge have fermented to digestion-helping perfection. Here are 10 more things that improve with maturity.

1 OUR ABILITY TO LIVE WITHOUT A SCALE.

We don't need to weigh in to know we're fine with our shape. How our clothes fit and the mirror do the real job. Our decision to not let ourselves totally go requires an understanding of the relationship between food, health, and self-esteem . . . and a desire to look good. We finally understand that a balanced diet keeps us mentally sharp and helps us manage health problems—big motivation here.

The idea of possible heart disease, stroke, high blood pressure, type-2 diabetes, bone loss, cancer, or anemia is enough to keep us disciplined about eating and exercise—even more than a sale rack of designer dresses.

When clothes feel tight we know it's time to eat smaller portions, and not in front of the TV or standing in front of the fridge at midnight. The calories in, calories out philosophy we lived by for so long doesn't really work when it comes to looking healthy. *What* we eat—not just the calorie count—makes the difference.

2 WE *REALLY* KNOW WHAT HAVING SENSITIVE SKIN MEANS.

Menopause does make our skin drier and more reactive.

Half the population of women 50+ claim to have sensitive skin and we should know! After years of using our faces as DIY science experiments for de-aging creams and treatments, we're experts on what makes us blotchy, red, rashy, and itchy. We're not being drama queens here, either, since menopause does make our skin drier and more reactive. By now those of us who are sensitive to retinol or AHAs, chemical sunscreens, and perfumed products know it and choose simple creams, sunscreens with zinc oxide and titanium oxide, and fragrance-free everything. Read the labels, girlfriends.

Test new skin and makeup products on the inside of an elbow for 48 hours before using. Just because a product says "dermatologist-tested" doesn't mean you won't develop a rash, itchiness, or sensitivity from some ingredient.

Tread carefully at nail salons, too. Make sure your nail salon cleanses foot basins with anti-fungal cleanser between clients; bring your own pumice stone and tools to prevent the spread of warts, foot fungus, nail infections, or super-bugs. Disgusting.

3 OUR MAKEUP APPLICATION SKILLS GET BETTER AND BETTER.

From covering circles to stippling on foundation, no one knows our faces the way we do. Makeup is easier than ever now as technology keeps improving texture, color, applicators, and tools to deal with pigmentation issues and loss of definition. Here are 3 things to try:

➤ **High-pigment makeup in sheer textures and serum-like formulas** in everything from foundations to blush and lipsticks for color and coverage without a heavy look (think watercolors rather than oil paint).

➤ **Gel eye pencils and waterproof kohl crayons** make lining close to the lashes and in the waterline easy and smear-proof.

➤ **Foundation and blender brushes** that leave no streaks and buff makeup and skin into one seamless unit.

We're eager to try whatever's new as more age-appreciative brands spotlight spokesmodels over 60 that aren't retouched to look like they're 35.

Marc Jacobs signed Jessica Lange at 64 to be the face of his Marc Jacobs Beauty brand campaign, François Nars signed 68-year-old Charlotte Rampling to front his 20th anniversary beauty campaign, and L'Oréal Paris has Diane Keaton at 66, Andie MacDowell at 56, Julianne Moore at 54, and Dame Helen Mirren at 65. Not bad. Now if only the rest of the beauty industry would embrace age diversity.

CAROL E. CAMPBELL

I like to maintain my weight, which has been pretty consistent since high school. But I'm a sugar fiend and carb addict—once I start with that stuff it's all over so I stay away from it. And as my friends like to say, "Carol eats large amounts of acceptable food." I hate portion control. If I like it, I like it! I work out because it empowers me and calms me down. I started doing Bikram yoga 4 years ago, when I got divorced, and it was a lifesaver. I also love horseback riding and got accepted into the 2015 NYC Marathon. What better time to try it than age 53? In some ways I feel like I look better now—emotionally and with knowledge I didn't have then.

4 WE BUY AND WEAR WHAT WE LOVE. WHENEVER. PERIOD.

We don't just buy what magazines say we should anymore. We develop long- and short-term affairs with what may or may not be *la mode* of the minute. Those of us who are fairly consistent in our choices say "I've found my look." We could change our mind tomorrow or wear the same look in 1,000 variations from now until forever.

The women in this book believe they can: still wear over-the-knee boots over skinny jeans or leggings, add a feathered toque for a drop-dead couture touch, do classic red nails that match top and bottom, wear turquoise tights to match a turquoise dress, toss on a bright pink shift and black patent Mary Janes and look womanly not girly and look awesome.

They buy everywhere from Walmart to Bloomingdale's, Joe Fresh to J. Crew, Bluefly to Barneys, consignment to couture to GoFetch.com, then mash it all together and make it look so individual, so them.

5 FASHION HAS NO SIZE LIMITATIONS.

The fashion industry's attitude has finally evolved—a little, at least. There are now trendy versions of everything in every size, although it's time to redefine "plus-size" or integrate it into regular sizing instead of sending women over a 12 off to fat-land fashion. The same goes for petites—aka women under 5 foot 4 inches. We are not "special sizes" categories; we're average. Women size 14 to 24 can finally find leather leggings, slim ankle pants, cashmere sweaters, and sheath dresses every bit as runway chic as sizes 00 to 12. I direct my curvy readers and clients to Violeta by Mango at mango.com, Eloquii at eloquii.com, and Asos Curve on asos.com. For petite women, Eileen Fisher at neimanmarcus.com and Topshop and MICHAEL Michael Kors at nordstrom.com.

According to the U.S. Center for Disease Control and Prevention—just FYI—we are 5 foot 4 inches or shorter, weigh between 150 and 160 pounds, and wear a size 14 on average. This, girlfriend, is the new normal.

AUDREY SMALTZ

Sexy is really an attitude. When I go out I like a tapered skirt and heels. Here's the secret to wearing heels painlessly: you have to find a shoe designer whose structure fits your foot—curves and supports your arch and foot shape exactly. Just because Christian Louboutin boots are trendy doesn't mean they'll work for you. I'm very loyal to Manolo Blahniks, which are expensive but fit me perfectly. I have dozens that have lasted for years with care. I get them resoled and baby them. The Manolo Carolyne pump in black or red is my basic, but I love the d'Orsay style, too.

6 OUR FAVORITE WARM NEUTRAL MAKEUP NEVER DISAPPOINTS.

No matter what the color trends, our warm neutral and "nude" makeup will survive. We appreciate their ability to enhance our maturing features and make us look better but not painted no matter how much brown eye shadow, coffee liner, or nude-toned lip color we apply. For the sake of "new," beauty companies disguise our beiges, camels, and earth tones with clever names like mushroom, cork, coconut, or latte, but the whole naked to brown palette is there and works for every skin tone, eye color, and hair color. Grab new multi-tasking palettes every season with multiple light to dark shades and textures, including sheer, matte, satin, and shimmery. Pick up liners from chocolate to espresso, mascaras in dark brown or brown-black (gentler than black now). They'll never fail us . . . even at 90.

7 WE LAYER UP THE WAY DERMATOLOGISTS DO.

After years of listening to dermatologists, we practically have medical degrees ourselves. Dermatologists now suggest multitasking skin products whenever possible to minimize the chance of overload and sensitivity. You might use one cream with moisturizers, peptides, hyaluronic acid, antioxidants, and broad-spectrum sunscreen, for example. However lots of us still prefer layering to achieve specific results. If you do:

➤ **Start with the lightest, thinnest products, like serums,** that deliver active concentrated ingredients into the skin efficiently. Give that layer a couple of minutes to absorb.

➤ **Tap on your eye cream next** at inner corners and crow's feet.

➤ **Lock it all down with a moisturizing cream** that contains humectants like hyaluronic acid and glycerin and antioxidants to hydrate dry skin and plump it up.

➤ **Add a botanical oil or oil blend** to add radiance as a touch-up anywhere skin is unusually dry. Oils can penetrate moisturizer, but not the other way around. Oils also work solo as a do-all treatment.

➤ **Last is sun protection** since it sits on top.

At nighttime, do the same but skip the sunscreen and add a retinol or night cream with peptides, vitamin C, or AHAs to firm, repair, and rebuild collagen.

8 WE REALIZE CHUNKY LEGS ARE OUR SIDEKICKS FOR LIFE.

Know what? We're fine with that. Those of us with heavy legs used to hate them and hide out in pants. Full thighs but slim legs knees down? No problem—wear whatever you like. Unlike tummies, we can't suck in big calves or cankles with shapewear or diet them off—they're hereditary. So learn to create an illusion of longer, slimmer legs. There are two issues women cite most: heavy calves and thick ankles, which make legs appear to lack definition or full calves and slim ankles which exaggerate the disparity. There are 4 tricks to improving your leg proportions:

➤ **Keep hemlines full at the knees** in A-line and pleated skirts and fit-and-flare dresses.

➤ **Stick to shoes with a lower vamp (the "neckline" on top) and tapered toes** regardless of heel height, and choose shoes in a shade that matches your skin tone for no obvious break where your leg ends and your shoe begins. Or . . . match your shoes/booties/boots to your tights.

➤ **A lower heel from kitten to a 2-incher,** substantial curvy "Louis" cone, stacked heels, and curvy contoured wedges give muscular legs balance and beauty.

➤ **When it comes to boots:** choose shoe-booties that dip below the ankle in front in a nude shade or black. For boot flattery, thick calves and slim ankles benefit from classic straight riding boots with full zips to the sole, for easy on-off or pull-on stretch boots in soft stretch suede. Heavy calves and thick ankles love motorcycle boots, and stretch leather or suede boots with elastic stretch panel inserts at the sides or back for ease and comfort.

9 YOUR BRA CHOICES.

We finally stopped trying to fit our 32DD chest into the same old 34B bra. Boobs change with age, bloat, and weight so get refitted and toss the old, stretched-out buggers. And remember mature breasts vary a lot in shape, fullness, proportions, position, and spacing even though thousands of us wear the same bra size. You want the least bra for maximum support and a sexy look, so never let bra fitters talk you into a big old-style "brassiere."

➤ **If your breasts droop,** the band or cups may be too big or you're wearing a do-nothing bra. Your bra should lift those girls up and off your midriff for youthful side and front views. Older boobs are often teardrop shaped and fuller at the bottom, so molded bras or foam-lined cups can provide a more rounded, even shape.

➤ **If your bra gives you double boobs** with spillage at the top, the cups are too small. Go up a size (or more) and choose full-coverage cups that enclose without squishing or squeezing.

➤ **If your bra gives you back fat or side boob bulges** in sleeveless dresses, try styles with a wider, soft band at the sides and back, or a T or racerback. Check your bra band and cups. They're probably too small.

➤ **If your underwires or bra back hike up** try a smaller band, bigger cups. Underwires should sit on your rib cage directly beneath your boobs. The band should feel snug when fastened on the loosest hook. Extra hooks are there to compensate for stretch and wear as time goes on.

10 YOUR PEER BOND AND SENSE OF COMMUNITY.

As major online shoppers, nothing pushes us to buy like positive detailed reviews from everyday women like us. Some department store sites like Nordstrom and Saks Fifth Avenue provide the age range of customers giving product reviews for beauty, clothing, and accessories and ask whether a specific review was helpful. Where site reviews do not include age, mention yours in your opinion. Do it! The more responsive we are as a group, the more opportunity for marketing teams to spot the need to highlight us and be more inclusive with *imaging* as well as opinions. Check which products and colors are selling with no complaints or returns before you hit "Add to Shopping Bag."

BROADMINDED: AN ATTITUDE ADJUSTMENT CHANGES EVERYTHING!

Get over it! If "quality of life" is your goal, you've got to lose the negative attitude. As I've said, I'm not a psychotherapist but from decades of working with women 50+ and listening to them in moods ranging from genial to gloomy, optimism is clearly the way to go. It helps us achieve goals, gets us over the bumpy spots, and affects our emotional and physical well-being—even reducing inflammation in the body (a major factor in aging well).

This is the time to refocus, find fresh solutions, and trust in yourself. Movement and laughter are a good place to start. Dance your butt off, sashay, swagger, and shake your booty, or just take a brisk walk to shake off your anger or darkness. Try to giggle once a day. I laugh at a lot of things—my "conversations" with my car "Blue-ie," while driving, at my inability to find Netflix, and my daughters' emergency fashion e-mails. ("Mom! Should I buy this?") Show a little self-love and humor when it comes to your looks and body. They have been on this journey with you through thick and thin, firm and saggy, brunette and blonde—whatever your transitions have been. Dress to express and keep experimenting. Aging is a confidential matter, how you look during the process isn't. C'mon:

STAY AN ALLURING ENIGMA.

Keeping things unsaid, holding something back, makes us fascinating to others. Silences don't always have to be filled with chatter. Get comfortable with not revealing all. How you feel about your own aging process is not up for discussion; neither is your de-aging strategy. Whether you do the health thing—running marathons, swilling greens, buying organic produce; the medi thing—face-lift, lasers, veneers; or the fake thing—spray tan, hair extensions, faux nails—feel free to keep it to yourself. Too much self-absorption and self-deprecating comments are turn-offs. If you dislike your upper arms, wax your lady bits into a heart, plan on getting your boobs lifted, or IPL therapy for sun damage—it's your private affair. Be vague when asked why you look so great. "I'm happy?" Don't be an approval seeker. Stay cool, calm, and composed.

GO TO YOUR SCHOOL REUNIONS.

We know we're the smartest, best-educated, most accomplished women our age ever in history, so why do high school, college, and grad reunions reduce us to nervous wrecks? Our jitters are enough to shake the sequins off a DVF dress. Of course, we're all older but you might be in for a few surprises . . . like that cheerleader frenemy who stole your boyfriend is not exactly the babe she was 40 years ago, or that guy who intimidated you but was your secret crush is now bald and boring. The cure for nerves? Five confidence-boosting tricks that work:

- **Start with a "light" full-body salon spray tan** by a technician who knows how to sculpt, tone legs and arms, and relax about skipped workouts—you'll look like an Olympic athlete when she's done.

- **Apply caffeine-packed skin serums or gel creams** to your tummy, jawline, and under-eye area to deflate puffiness. It acts like a diuretic to suck excess fluid out. Use an eye cream on facial areas, a body cream down below to reduce bloat.

- **Dab Visine on broken capillaries** on a last-minute zit and under-eye circles. It's a vaso-constrictor so it takes away redness and discolorations.

- **Take a short warm bath after you apply makeup.** The hint of steam takes the excess makeup edge off, sets it, and plumps up lines.

- **Apply an essential oil instead of a primer** or moisturizer under makeup.

- **Blend a luminzer liquid with your foundation** for extra glow.

- **Whiten your teeth.** Splurge on a pre-event in-office procedure if you haven't been doing whitening strips at home.

- **Color your nails.** Do a salon mani/pedi in a classy red or edgy dark color.

- **Wear a dress in red or white**—2 skin brightening, lively colors that are easy to spot in a crowd of black in your favorite dress silhouette (sheath, shift, or fit and flare).

- **Add heels**—they're a must, even low ones.

MAKE PANTS YOUR THING.

If you're into comfort, have no real need for dresses, or just prefer pants, you can get away with living in them 24/7. They're the great equalizer—feminine and powerful and clearly work for Ellen DeGeneres and Hillary Clinton. There are a lot of style, fabric, and proportion options but jeans, slim ankle pants, tailored slouchy pants, and even leggings (which count as pants now) get you through any situation and climate.

Don't ignore vintage menswear when scouting consignment shops, flea markets, and vintage sites. Beautifully hand-tailored jackets—especially riding jackets, alligator belts, vintage trench coats, striped shirts, cardigans, tweed topcoats, caps, and scarves made for him mixed with your jeans, leggings, or ankle pants makes for personal style. Just add ballet flats, heels, or booties for charm.

MYRNA BLYTH

Adding one trendy item can make even classic clothes look newly fashionable. For a recent AARP Movies for Grownups gala in L.A. where everyone—top stars, assorted directors, writers, and producers showed up—I bought a gold Topshop jacket that I wore over a black camisole-like top and a black skirt and it looked good. I felt great and movie-star-ish in it.

CHAPTER SEVEN

HOW NOT TO BE INVISIBLE

BECAUSE TO PARAPHRASE CARLY SIMON, "WE'RE SO VAIN."

We *still* crave the brief boost of an appreciable knowing look from total strangers. This is a healthy form of narcissism. Our educated and enriched generation of women has always felt smarter—and more smug about being so—than any other in history. We like to think of ourselves as intelligent, attractive, centered, accomplished, optimistic, sexy, and well . . . attractive. But mostly we like to think we're heading in the right direction as we age. Hopefully, we'll stay fit in mind and body and socially connected. But back to that ego boost. If we still look appealing and feel youthful, why aren't we getting the reactions now that we got at 30? Not even getting them from men our age? The #1 reason is that everyone is on their phone while they go about their business, and so are you! No one looks up. In our glory days, we'd walk into a restaurant, airport lounge, waiting room, or stride down the street and actually exchange looks with people, smile, or at least acknowledge one another. The fish guy at Whole Foods would smile

AUDREY SMALTZ

Know who you are! I'm not a Boomer, not a senior. I'm a woman of a certain hip age! When you know who you are, you don't have to wear what's in fashion, you wear what looks good on *you* and when you've got it right, believe me you're not invisible. Color near my face is good for me. I like colorful leather jackets and colorful tunics with black pants and form-sitting dresses. Don't be afraid to make dramatic hair color changes, either. I *had* to go blonde—that headband of silver was driving me crazy as a redhead.

back at us and the valet parking attendant would call us honey, not ma'am. Despite an enviable list of accomplishments, admirable skills, and plenty of charisma, lots of women 50+ say they no longer get second glances . . . or even eye contact from people . . . and that bugs us.

> Start thinking of yourself as a superstar, you need to ace this life performance now.

BRENDA COFFEE

Like many women 50+, I feel invisible. While it's disconcerting, the one thing that bothers me most is my neck! I've never tried Botox, much less a face-lift, but I think about it . . . a lot. Until a few years ago I wore contacts, now I wear updated glasses. My hair is a priority since it's very fine since chemo and estrogen loss. A fabulous stylist and colorist are my monthly splurge to maximize my visibility. Since we're the wealthiest demographic, I want all top beauty and fashion brands to show they care about more than just my wallet. A megabrand recently told me that women over 40 are no longer relevant. Grrr . . . I use "Grrr" as a substitute for the string of bad words that are just dying to roll off my tongue.

AGE IS APPROPRIATE AND AWESOME

Yes the technology obsession is not helping, but don't blame your age! Whether you get someone's attention has more to do with unconsciously dressing for "invisibility." In our youth- and celebrity-based society, everyone under 50 wants to be a star. So be honest. You think slapping on a baseball cap and slapdash layers of clothes that totally hide your shape is alluring? Combine *that* with our own smartphone hunch as we text or read e-mails everywhere we go. And wonder why you have "tech neck" crinkles? How can you bewitch anyone when you're sabotaging yourself? Tired of the word reinvention? Let's skip straight to something manageable and doable, like your appearance and attitude. Start thinking of yourself as a superstar, the prima ballerina, the diva in *Carmen* or *The Merry Widow*, because you need to ace this life performance now. You don't have 30 years to rehearse. You're about to step onstage.

LET'S DISH

We have varying degrees of chutzpah but all mature women have it. I grew up hearing that Yiddish word for confidence as a compliment, though some seem to think it hints at behavior going beyond typical or acceptable. The way I see it, having a little backbone and brass is a good thing. You can't be visible unless you're seen and heard! Everyday courage—even in small doses—creates windows of opportunity and strengthens our resolve to tackle bigger life issues.

At 50+, you need nerve to saunter sarong-free down the beach in a bikini, to strip down to your birthday suit for a bikini wax, strut to the office in leather leggings . . . when your conscience says wear a black one-piece, trim your lady bits at home, and can't you wear a dress like everyone else?

You've got to be gutsy to train for a marathon, book an adventure trek across the desert on a camel when your inner voice is saying . . . please just go to the gym or can't you just do a Jane Fonda video? It takes balls to disagree with your boss in a meeting, tell your husband you're filing for divorce, or make demands to a landlord. Women who are high-visibility are not the walking-on-eggshells type. We're not shy whether we blog our views to an audience of thousands, chair a conference of industry leaders, or confront a best friend in need of an intervention. And just remember: to be the smartest, most attractive, dynamic, and fascinating woman in the room, all you need is to believe that you are.

ALISON HOUTTE

I believe you have to create sexy. No grandma panties. My 4 sisters think I'm crazy with my lingerie collection but it sets the tone! As a model I wore a one-piece vintage leopard bodysuit to a commercial callback and got the job! Buying vintage definitely projects attitude. You're wearing something one-of-a-kind and eye-catching! Any 1950s vintage black evening dress will look like you're wearing current couture, anything vintage leopard or Pucci-esque makes you stand out. And they are conversation starters.

....

Q: How do I get the courage from
my brain to take action?

A: Face your fears in baby steps:
today a red lipstick, next week a new hair color,
next month your high school reunion,
and maybe a little shot of Botox confidence.

Feeling skeptical about still fitting in if you stand out too much? Ignore it. Having the guts to be conspicuous is how actresses win film roles, athletes get gold medals, and politicians get elected. Unless you're unusually eccentric in dress and manner, it's not a problem. Keep your sense of humor and ability to laugh at yourself going—it's how the movers and shakers of the world get through every day. Socializing in a crowd is easy—everyone else is too busy "connecting" to notice your anxiety. Just don't make a habit of hiding in the ladies' room.

....

BEEN THERE, DONE THAT

It dawned on me one day standing in line for my usual nonfat skinny vanilla latte, that I was the oldest person there. The barista guy didn't even look up when he asked for my order or name. Tempted to say Bette Midler or Jessica Lange, I wondered whether I'd be forced to get my a.m. energizer at the local bakery, where dozens of gray-haired babes with walkers congregated. It must be my voice or my age-giveaway hands, because the rest of me rocked (or at least I thought so!). Wearing trendy jeans and harness booties, a relaxed tee and sweater, a slouchy beanie on my jagged blonde bob, pastel aviators, I felt like the cool girl in the clique in my head but knew I was being viewed as the mother/grandmother I am. There is a line between "them" and us when it comes to twenty- and thirty-somethings. Remember they come from a different planet, where the moment exists only on Instagram or Twitter. Oddly enough, when I'm with my peers I feel like there is always a connection because "someone's home." So what did I do? Exactly as I suggest in my tips to follow!

LOIS'S TUTORIAL OF TRICKS #7

We're not movie stars, TV stars, or even tabloid stars who get ambushed by paparazzi every time we venture out. But we certainly don't want to get lost in the crush at work, business-related events, parties, or reunions and we certainly don't want to be ignored by sales associates, flight attendants, salon managers, or get elbowed out of the way in a mob at the movies, a concert, stadium game, flea market, or the mall. There's a little bit of diva in all of us.

1 SPEAK UP! LAUNCH A CONVERSATION OR DIVE INTO ONE.

Don't just hang out looking great or melt silently into a group of people. Plunge ahead. Add your voice, opinions, laughter, and spirit to ongoing discussions. Ask questions of strangers. If you're not exactly up on the topic, you'll learn something new; if you do have something to add, you'll light up the dialogue. Initiate conversations, but no more "What do you do?" or "How's your day going?" These are dead-end questions.

People are always flattered by another person's interest in them, their knowledge, past, or experience.

It can be as broad as "So what's your story?" or as specific as "Where do you love to go on vacation—I can't decide and have a week off?" Start talking to people everywhere—in the next seat at the movies, ask the couple next to you what they ordered at a restaurant, stop someone on the street to ask where they bought that fabulous coat. Once you become a conversation addict, you'll feel like a talk show host 24/7.

2 SPOIL YOURSELF.

If you treat yourself like a superstar, it begins to stick inside. Start the day at a coffee bar to perk you right up in a social environment. Of course, you can make coffee or tea at home but a vanilla chai latte, espresso, or decadent caramel macchiato and an interesting soul at the next table make it worth going out. Talk to the guy in the Barbour jacket with a stack of real newspapers (why isn't *he* at home reading them?!) or the two women having an animated conversation over chocolate croissants. Ask who does their hair color and say you're looking for a new local salon. Splurge on one extra bonus item a week—a new bar of scented soap, a pack of imported breath mints, a travel tube of hand cream, a fresh pair of tights. Drugstores, beauty shops, and health-food stores are havens of pamper picks.

A little self-indulgence makes us feel invincible. And for those of us really into instant-gratification, few things make us happier than walk-in blow-out bars.

No distraction of cuts or color, an in-and-out policy of 30 to 40 minutes, and a pro blow-out that lasts 3 days. You'll feel like a movie star, which is why some of us are making this a once-a-week habit, especially when we're having some major medical/family/work/relationship stress. Nirvana. And get yourself a blowout before asking for a raise, going on a first date, any party, event, or occasion where an ego boost can't hurt.

3 WEAR ONE SHOW-OFF THING EVERY DAY.

Get out of your comfort zone and add a trend-of-the minute item or a distinctive or colorful accessory. I guarantee you won't go unnoticed. Stylish attention-getters vary according to your own gutsy approach but might include: one cubic zirconia ear cuff or big dangly ethnic earrings, a man-style fedora, glasses in a startling color, a vintage shoulder bag dripping in fringe. Expect compliments, questions, and comments because you'll get them.

CAROL E. CAMPBELL

If you do the best you can with what you have that's sexy and will get attention. That will make you feel good about yourself, which makes you confident, which gets more attention. I do feel the need to stay on top of age-appropriate trends but I can wear over-the-knee boots with leather leggings— at least I think I can!

4 GO "LIGHT."

Women who carry multiple bags or gigantic bags filled with every emergency item they could possibly need, are never going to be the heroines of their own lives. Aside from the practical points—like sliding through crowds and lines, managing graceful introductions and kiss-kiss greetings with a free hand, lugging a lot of baggage dims your wattage. It makes us appear anxious, nervous, heavier (all those bags bulk up our silhouette and wreck our posture).

Successful women carry very little and always in small to medium bags. They trust they'll get through without backup and look cool.

They leave duplicates of essentials at home, the office, and health club. They have all info and apps on tiny tech gadgets (so no lugging big totes jammed with folders, files, and magazines anymore). After all, you can pick up anything extra, from fold-up ballet flats to bras and snacks at the drugstore now!

5 WEAR MORE SKIRTS, DRESSES, AND BLOUSES.

Just because we live in a country where jeans and T-shirts are the official dress code doesn't mean you have to play by the rules. Try giving your sporty basic wardrobe a major feminine jolt. Pair jeans with flow-y silk blouses and embellished shoes. Swap out leggings for trim tailored ankle pants and wear them with V-neck cashmere sweaters, long necklaces, and loafers for a very European kind of chic. Wear feminine print shirts and skirts that flare as if they were jeans and pair them with ballet flats and boots. It's a softer approach to style that sets you apart without looking dowdy or schoolgirl-y.

6 HAVE A TROPHY MAN ON SPEED DIAL.

We don't need a CEO or movie star on our arm. However, in certain situations—like when you RSVP'd for 2 to a dinner party, gala, or wedding—an attractive man with lots of personality can add something—could be an ex, your brother, the divorced architect who renovated your kitchen, or your uncle Jeremy. Age doesn't matter but maintenance and hygiene do. Nice teeth, hair that rocks (anything from Brad Pitt long, Denzel Washington cropped, to Bruce Willis shaved), clean nails, and a great laugh are more important than designer clothes or a hot car.

7 SHOW UP LAST.

Not late, of course, just be the last one there but still on time. Whether it's for meetings, lunches, or parties you'll make an entrance like an award winner winding toward the stage. Funny but our generation is the last to wear watches or own clocks, even alarm clocks! Everyone else checks the time on their cell or tablet and sets their phone for wake-ups. "I'm running late" is now actually not only an acceptable text or e-mail to get but it's the new normal. "See you at 7:30" now means you'll leave the house or office at that time and arrive "traffic was horrendous!" 20 minutes past. Everyone assumes you have an exciting, jam-packed life and theirs by comparison is dull, expected, and boring.

8 KNOW THE NEWEST ROLL AND WRAP STYLING TRICKS.

There are 3 things we can all revise without watching a YouTube video. One of the most deadly don'ts in styling is cuffing your sleeves and pants incorrectly, the other is wearing a scarf like a neck brace.

➤ **To roll cotton and denim button-down sleeves like a stylist,** turn back the cuff and sleeve up to your elbow, then roll the remaining bottom part of the sleeve up toward the elbow but leave the cuff free. Roll the bottom of the sleeve up one more time and gently tug the outside corner of the cuff so it pokes out. Push the sleeve up the arms so the cuff sits right above the elbow. If you add a sweater or cardigan on top, push the sleeves of that up to your elbow first and then roll the sleeves of the shirt as above.

➤ **To make long scarves less bulky,** when you do the fold in half and pull both ends through the loop thing, don't. Instead fold the scarf in half as usual but slip only one end through the loop, then knot with the other; much less bulky especially under jackets or if you have a short neck.

➤ **To style up jeans, just roll the bottoms—** don't fold them—to just above the anklebone, *not* consciously matched, uniform, and neatly folded. The roll should be roughly an inch wide. This gives boyfriend jeans a feminine tweak as you reveal your slim ankles in heels, booties, flats, or sneakers. This is a gift for shorter women who never have to get their jeans hemmed again!

9 LOOK SENSATIONAL AT THE GYM.

You think no one's watching because they're too busy huffing and puffing and doing their own crunches and lunges? Lauren Hutton once told me she always meets guys at the gym. Wear fitted black and gray workout clothes that show your shape—that's shape, not skin. Wear a good sports bra with cup separation so your boobs stay a duo and stationary under a racerback tank or tee—not the sports bra alone. Skip leggings and yoga pants that are too thin and sheer. You want opacity, a higher waistband, and hold; no one needs to see your booty crack or skin peering through fabric. Wear track pants or fashion sweatpants, or casual fold-over knit pants if you're running errands after or before. Gap, Victoria's Secret, and Old Navy have great fashionable low-cost versions. Add a sweatshirt, hoodie, or nylon zip-up for cover after.

Get your hair up off your face and neck to get a look going—add a wide black stretchy hairband if you have bangs or short hair, twist longer hair into a pony, bun, or knot. Take off your makeup with wipes. After your workout, mist your roots with dry shampoo to suck up scalp oil and freshen and then redo the pony, bun, or knot and tousle shorter hair. Splash your face with cold water and add a tinted moisturizer—your skin will be glowing form the workout. And that endorphin high will last.

10 CHANGE YOUR HAIR COLOR.

Want to get attention? Brad Johns of the Brad Johns Color Studio at the Samuel Shriqui Salon in NYC says, "Changing your hair color is a big wham! Like buying a painting for an empty wall." Consider this eye-catching tweak an investment in your looks. Brad suggests we "leave it up to a pro to manipulate warm or cool shades that will compensate for age-related hair and skin changes. For blonde to brunette or vice versa, a gradual transformation over several visits is safer for your hair. Correcting hair that's over-bleached or too dark takes time, and a pro can vary tones with highlights for a natural look that's more youthful than solid color. Even dark brunettes benefit from a few lighter brown highlights in the caramel, butterscotch, amber range."

Actresses Jane Seymour, Raquel Welch, Jaclyn Smith, and Susan Sarandon have warmed up their dark brown hair. The gradual brown to blonde strategy worked for *Vogue* editor Anna Wintour, while born brunettes Madonna, Barbra Streisand, and Jane Fonda are blonder than ever. Brad says, "Women go blonde at 50+ because it makes them feel younger, sexier, more fashionable. When a blonde walks into a room with two brunettes, the blonde—being the brightest—visually gets noticed first." So chums, put your money into your hair color, the accessory you never take off.

SASS TALK: PAY ATTENTION TO US, SALESPEOPLE! WE HAVE MONEY!

One of our pet peeves when it comes to stores is beauty and fashion sales associates who have no interest in helping anyone our age. They're always on their Bluetooth (that is, if they're not busy talking to one another). Helloooo! We have money to burn—actually women 55+ control three-fourths of America's wealth. Why are we instantly directed to de-aging products, stuffy labels, and loose boxy styles? Maybe we just want a new smoky kohl pencil or a dress "like the one *you're* wearing" or gold gladiator sandals? And don't let salespeople steer you to "mature" brands. Maybe you want to check out indie or edgy ones like Sunday Riley, Hourglass, Rag & Bone, or Topshop. We want positive imaging online, in ads, and store displays. We outspend younger women in stores and online. According to the U.S. Government Consumer Expenditure Survey, women 50+ spend $21 billion annually *just on clothes*.

JUST BETWEEN US:
10 THINGS THAT GIVE US CONFIDENCE

Of course, self-esteem doesn't sprout from a face-lift or carrying a Gucci bag, though either one often gives some women a well-meaning shove in that direction. But are you getting any compliments lately? You do realize that in order for that to happen you have to be noticeable. How you behave, dress, talk, and, of course, what you contribute socially and at work matters. If you think the grass is going to turn instantly greener if you had enough money to buy the things that make rich and famous women "stars," forget it. The secret to being conspicuous, eye catching, distinctive, outstanding, notable, and spectacular is not about cosmetic surgery, designer labels, or a fancy title.

1 LISTEN TO EMPOWERING MUSIC.

Whatever does it for you—anything from Beyoncé to Alicia Keys, Carla Bruni, Etta James, or Aretha Franklin. Thanks to Spotify and our iPods, we can take our inspiration with us for a fast fix anywhere. Your most liberating sounds might be nature, Gregorian chants, Handel, or the Beach Boys. Solo listening is the best therapy, your private morale-booster. But some of us might like a more public performance and pump up by singing in a choir or belting out your heart at a karaoke bar with the girls. Whenever my daughter Jen and I are in the car together we sing . . . though we're both tone deaf.

2 TAKE A SELF-DEFENSE CLASS.

Having a sense of personal security builds self-assurance—you become your own bodyguard. We may not be as strong, or move as fast as we did at 30 but we can be more aware and able to take charge in dangerous situations. Most women 50+ spend time walking alone, in parks, around their neighborhood, in parking lots . . . sometimes at night or early morning and often on the phone or lost in thought. You'll never feel vulnerable if your street smarts include a few learned moves that could disable an attacker and allow you to get away. While women immediately think "martial arts" (which can improve cardio and mobility), know that judo involves a lot of grappling, tackling, and falling down, taekwando uses a lot of head-high spinning kicks, and karate involves a lot of chops that our bone-weakened hands may not be up for. My favorite is Krav Maga, an Israeli self-defense technique designed for quick street fighting. A powerful, brutal kick to the groin, a double poke in the eyes, and you can incapacitate your attacker long enough to run for help.

3 LOOK LIKE YOU'RE HAVING THE TIME OF YOUR LIFE.

Laughing, talking, and moving your face advertises your sex appeal. Yes, sometimes a little play-acting is necessary but if stars can do it, so can we. Lose your inhibitions by imagining you are the celebrity of your choice. Four energizers help:

➤ **Get some fresh air**—even 10 to 20 minutes of brisk walking revs you up.

➤ **Snack on protein and healthy fats**—peanut butter on a slice of apple, a small handful of nuts.

➤ **Get a kick from a cup of caffeine or cold water.** Just press cold, damp hands to made-up cheeks to revive your looks.

➤ **Stretch**—a warm-up even in the ladies room gets you up.

4 SHIMMER IN SOME WAY EVERY DAY.

Amp up the wattage so you sparkle. You don't need diamonds to catch the spotlight.

➤ **A hint of luminizer/highlighting cream** on the top ledge of cheekbones or mixed with your everyday foundation does it.

➤ **Golden-flecked finishing cream or mist** for hair does it, too.

➤ **Gold or silver foil metallic nail polish** or a glittery topcoat over any color.

➤ **Subtle sheer shimmery shadows** layered over neutral matte eye makeup (swiped on lightly like fairy dust) brightens tired eyes.

➤ **Mirror finish loafers,** jewel-trimmed ballet flats, or sandals add a bolt of light to everyday wardrobes (always look for these at post-holiday and summer sales when they pop up).

5 KEEP TAKING RISKS. DARE YOURSELF.

You don't have to swim from Florida to Cuba without a shark cage (as Diana Nyad did at 64 and bravo for her!), but you could skinny-dip in the ocean or a lake at night. Try zip-lining or adopt a shelter dog on the kill-list just in time. Take yourself out to dinner solo at the hottest new restaurant and eat at the bar, or go to the movies, a concert, a sports event . . . alone. Spend a year taking cooking classes—Italian, Latin, Vietnamese—which will improve your own foodie know-how and make you an outstanding restaurant-going date. You can even sign on to work a cruise ship and get a genuine lifestyle change and the promise of adventure. All you need to do is be fit and healthy enough to work 10-hour days, 7 days a week, for as long as 6 months at a stretch and possibly be willing to share a cabin with another crew member.

RENE SYLER

Be your true self and you'll stand out in a crowd. My hair makes a statement. My crazy curls fit my personality and for the first time in my life, I truly love my hair. I spent three decades using chemicals and heat to straighten it the way other African American female news anchors wore their hair. Finally I said no more! I wasn't going to try to fit a standard of beauty I wasn't meant to be. Now this hair is my signature. Being confident and happy with your body empowers you and allows you to really be yourself.

6 BOOK A SALON MASSAGE.

The touch of another person in the totally non-sexual, professional environment of a day spa is healing and can provide an emotional release for those feeling insecure or hesitant. First tip longtime divorced or widowed women tell newbies is to sign up for a series of weekly massages. Aside from relaxing your muscles and lowering your heart rate, massage can soothe away headaches, fatigue, back and neck pain, and help relieve depression.

In this screen-to-screen universe, where human contact is becoming less frequent, the hands-on experience makes a difference to those needing an esteem boost. Even working with a personal trainer, getting a pedicure and manicure, or a blow-out pumps up our self-respect muscle. It connects us in a non-threatening way to other people and that keeps us feeling seen.

7 GET A PRO SPRAY TAN.

Think about a.m. talk show hosts, financial analysts, and news anchors now. They wear "party" hair at dawn, makeup I'd wear to a Hollywood premiere, and dresses that would work for cocktails. Of course, it's for the camera but what really makes the difference in these HD days is a salon spray tan head-to-toe instead of body makeup. DIY self-tanners are fine for every day, but major events, beach, or sexy moments call for a salon spray tan. The difference? A pro blurs skin discolorations right down to your toes in a creamy, uniform hue including *every* nook and cranny. Do a salon spray tan 2 days before whatever is making you jumpy to give the color time to settle. Moisturize like crazy. And remember, you still just want to bump up your skin tone, not go for a dark tanned look.

8 WEAR COLORS THAT SAY "JUST WATCH ME!"

Two birds arrive at the feeder hanging from your deck, a brown wren and a red robin. Which one catches your eye? Never mind the psychological and physical impact of going outside your comfort zone, but dressing in color makes you memorable to others, too. These 5 work especially well for us:

➤ **Any shade of red** heats up your look and attitude and works like a charge of adrenaline. It's intense, gives you high visibility, and sends a fiery message of strength and energy. Red is great for public speaking, crammed parties, events, or luncheons where we're competing for attention.

➤ **Deep rich blues** like navy, indigo, and French blue (a sort of lapis lazuli jewel-tone) are soothing, calming, and inspire trust. They're as slimming as black and easy to find in tailored clothes and softer tops like blouses, tees, and sweaters. Wear this hue for interviews, first meetings of any kind, and uncomfortable situations (court, prenup discussions, and negotiating a raise or promotion).

➤ **Green** is restful and reduces anxiety (which is why you often see it in clinics and hospitals). The easiest, most tranquil shades to wear are natural earthy greens like olive, hunter, and soft gray-greens like moss and celadon. Wear green in stressful workplaces, during times of crisis, and when doing volunteer work. It has a self-reliant vibe that's reassuring, too.

➤ **Pink** makes a feminine "up" statement but also radiates health and romance. Sophisticated shades like rose or sunny coral-pink, bright "fashion" pinks, and even almost nude shades brighten your looks. They have the same effect as red but on a more subdued level. Wear pink for dating (even in small doses like a print scarf or a tee), when recovering from an illness, for reunions, and birthdays.

➤ **White** makes a cool, pragmatic impact and radiates light so we feel cleaner, more alert, and look authoritative (why it's favored for doctors and nurses). Crisp white shirts and new tees give any wardrobe a new look, as does a tailored white blazer or dress. Wear white when you feel drab, tired, and dull. It rejuvenates in seconds even without makeup.

MAURY ROGOFF

Sexy? So rarely do I feel that way. No, I'm not completely at peace about my age. But my hard-earned gold Bulgari watch and Fendi croc tote (bought at final sale markdown) still make me feel great decades later and instead of Armani suits I wear them with dresses by Zara, DVF, Milly, and Haute Hippie, feeling stylish, pulled together, and current.

9 BE AN INTERESTING PERSON.

That's the essential thing that gives us confidence. According to dermatologist Dr. Jeannette Graf, "Most women seeking rejuvenation come in for a consultation and aren't sure what they want. Fillers are expensive and when I tell patients the cost of a syringe, they expect perfection from one syringe and frankly that's not possible."

The question becomes how much are you willing to spend to look and feel good? If a woman is starting life over again—maybe after divorce or dating for the first time in years, I always suggest she make changes in her lifestyle first. Be an interesting person: take a theater class, go to art galleries, a lecture, be approachable, and meet like-minded people. That's more important.

[If a woman is starting life over again, I always suggest she make changes in her lifestyle first.]

10 ADD A LITTLE SPARKLE.

Last, but not least, buy yourself a really good piece of jewelry. A pair of diamond-studded hoops never misses!

BROADMINDED: DIY ILLUSIONS CAN SAVE YOU!

Smoke and mirrors is a metaphor for something a little shady. Originally it referred to business transactions; now it's used in beauty and fashion speak when a little sleight of hand helps. Well, I'm all for it! Blurring flaws that bug you and improving on what you have or don't sounds logical to me.

Of course, no one wants to be the woman who comes home, takes off her makeup, hair extensions, shapewear, heels, and is totally unrecognizable as the person who walked in the door! But everyone uses a little practical magic these days. Great chefs enhance the taste of pretty basic food with artistic arrangements and one offbeat ingredient, realtors give homes for sale curb-appeal by staging them with rented furniture, and even major performers get help from backup singers and dancers, lighting, and special effects. And to paraphrase the legendary magazine editor who started *Cosmopolitan* magazine and wrote *Sex and the Single Girl* back in the day, Helen Gurley Brown, "Nearly every glamorous, wealthy successful career woman you might envy started out as some kind of schlep." So there.

USE PRIMERS TO IMPROVE MAKEUP YOU OWN.

You can make better use of the makeup sitting on your vanity with these helpers. Think of them as underwear. There are no-color primers that create a silky or velvety layer, blur-makers that work like a soft-focus lens, radiance boosters with light shimmer that provide a luminous lining or work as mixer to blend with your face makeup to increase glow. Some primers in bronze shades color-correct by adding to warmth or a sunny lit-from-within look to sallow, pasty, or ashy skin tones. Some also have moisturizing benefits and a broad-spectrum sunscreen for baseline protection. They all help whatever face makeup you currently use apply and blend more easily, wear longer. Eye shadow primers keep liners from smearing and shadows from disappearing or creasing. Pat it on lids and under the eyes to smooth the way for concealer and lock it in. You can use face or eye primers on your lips, too, to keep color from feathering or migrating into lines.

APPLY EYE MAKEUP UNDER YOUR GLASSES.

Statement glasses are priority accessories when you want to be noticed but load up on eyeliner for definition behind the lenses. It makes a difference to mature eyes. This is especially true if you have light colored eyes and lashes, which totally disappear.

➤ **Farsighted lenses are convex, so they magnify eyes and make them appear larger** but they also magnify flaws like crepey lids. If this is you, don't overdo the concealer but apply liner at the lash line, right between the roots and in the waterline inside the lids.

➤ **Nearsighted lenses are concave and make eyes appear smaller,** so intensify definition with liner and shadows to enlarge and contour a bigger shape (pale nude or sand shadow on lids, taupe or medium brown shadow in the crease, darkest liner at lash line).

SHOW OFF YOUR NECK, ARMS, AND LEGS; KEEP YOUR MIDDLE TO YOURSELF.

Let's be honest, a waist does add body definition but if your torso won't cooperate with crunches get it elsewhere—like displaying your shoulders, legs, or arms. Instead of worrying about everything in the middle, highlight your extremities. These will always be the thinnest parts of your body no matter what your size or weight. They give you an elegant, feminine look similar to the way the graceful arms and legs of a Louis XV chair frame the broad seat and back. Keep the ornamentation on target with bracelets, shoes with an unexpected pop of color, and a neckline that dips to reveal your collarbones. Choose straight shift dresses, especially prints that wriggle and squiggle in a haphazard way (not horizontal striped or rigid geometric patterns), tunic-cut shirts and sweaters over slim pants and jeans.

ADD FAKE HAIR TO MAKE-BELIEVE FAST.

Don't say no until you try a hairpiece, extension, or fake ponytail. Fake hair is the ultimate shortcut. It clips on in minutes, looks authentic, and cool and is a new solution for being conspicuous in a good way. I wore one of Christie Brinkley's faux ponytails (from her Christie Brinkley Hair2Wear Collection) to lunch with friends and felt sexy, youthful, and certainly distinctive. It's become my new "toy." Attaching the 30-inch tail to my own puny 2-inch pony took 60 seconds. Using wigs and pieces to transform your hair saves you on rainy days when frizz is a factor, or when your hair is a mess, dirty, and disheveled with no time for a shampoo. It also lets us keep experimenting risk-free with hair the way we do with clothes and makeup. In fact, if you're thinking about a major style or color change, this is the way to go first. Seek out synthetic hair—even wigs—with modern details like long feathery bangs, textured ends, layers, and color that is multi-tone for an authentic look. Faux hair can be thrown in a drawer or suitcase, shaken out, and plopped on for parties, meetings, and any social occasion when you want to get noticed.

USE TEXTURED POLISH FOR NAIL REHAB.

Manicures and pedicures can camouflage nails that are discolored, chipping, peeling, and weak. Just file and buff into a uniform shape and apply metallic, glittery, or matte polish in layers for the color, texture, and coverage you want. Dark or bold nails also divert attention from veins and brown spots on the backs of your hands and pull it toward your fingers and rings. Slather hands pre-manicure in microwave-warmed hand or body cream (not hot!) and swaddle in plastic wrap for a hand "facial." Be sure to dab opaque waterproof concealer like Dermablend on major brown spots post-mani. If you need to keep hands boardroom polished, choose unexpected new neutrals like gray, greige (that halfway color between nude and gray), or a very dark classic hue like navy, chocolate brown, inky plum, or blackened red.

SEIZE CONTROL.

Buy fresh power undies to compress, smooth, hold, and empower you with an immediate boost. There have been lots of updates to basic shapewear that make them more functional but sexy.

Bodysuits now have lacy power mesh insets with extra hold that look like a fancy part of the design. There are also open-bust bodysuits compatible with any bra for women who have larger boobs yet like the full coverage of a shoulder-to-thigh control garment.

Full-coverage T-shirt bras have more front closures for no visible bra bumps, thinner foam cups that don't feel too padded or push "the girls" up, and contoured racerbacks for comfort.

Shaper shorts now have more compression but in lighter fabrics (something like the idea of sheer high-pigment makeup), more 4-way stretch comfort with thinner power yarns for less bulk, and come in extended capri length to wear under pants or jeans.

Control panties are elastic-free but are waist-high with opaque compression panel fronts and lacy cheeky rears and total butt coverage.

Boy shorts offer minimal shaping but more than a typical panty and are wedgie-proof.

Cuchini Camel Toe Guard can prevent wedgies and visible splits in tight jeans, leggings, and swimsuits.

CHAPTER EIGHT

YOUR BEAUTY AND STYLE BUCKET LIST

YOU MADE IT!

Half a century of time travel got us to this fork in the road. We've learned the clichés: this is not a dress rehearsal, life's too short, emphasize the positive, live for today, and find an interest or passion that will last . . . blah blah blah. All totally true! And we've gotten over the "nice-girls-don't" thing. We do bleach the hell out of our hair if we feel like it and wear ripped-knee jeans. We've learned to resist woo-woo answers—no more calling psychics or relying on an astrology column for direction. We also don't get taken in by fashion trends, gobbling up the designer decree and fad of the moment like M&Ms. We *have* picked up a lot of miscellaneous practical advice along the way. For example: Pinterest can help us decide to go minimalist or country French in our new condo; never to bring a "fake" designer bag through customs (don't ask!); and $900 designer heels on sale for $190 that hurt at the sale will not "stretch" with time. Even though we feel healthy, energetic, and youthful, our face, hair, and body are tattletales, revealing stuff we don't want to share. Know what? We don't have to.

NANCY GANZ STEIR

I'm thinking about learning some simple code; HTML or JAVA script or maybe just how to make an app! I do have an idea for an upcoming project that is a culmination of my many passions: being part of a start-up, working with bright new entrepreneurs, a brick-and-mortar operation promoting healthy living along with implementing up-to-date technology.

AGE IS APPROPRIATE AND AWESOME

We buy products by the billions to improve our looks. As the largest, most affluent spenders on beauty, our influence changed the category formerly known as de-aging or anti-aging to age-enhancing. Nice going! Getting an entire industry to use positive language instead of what we considered ageist is why we're seeing words and phrases like volumizing, filling, hydrating, evens skin tone, restores radiance, and texture perfector. There's less mention of saggy skin, wrinkles, and brown spots. And . . .

LET'S DISH

Old thinking used to mean at some point we'd pull up our roots and melt into a retirement community somewhere like Florida or Arizona and be done. Well, we're not. More women 50+ are "aging in place" or placing a priority on new experiences and lifestyle changes that will revitalize their everyday lives.

Most of us now think of anything we do to look better—short of surgery—as the new normal.

There's been a huge shift in attitudes toward things like Botox and fillers. Most of us now think of anything we do to look better—short of surgery—as the new normal.

MORE OF US LEAPING AHEAD INTO THE FUTURE ARE:

USING COSMETIC DERMATOLOGY.

Mother Nature sure has a dark sense of humor. Just when we peak in personality and confidence, she sends us thinning hair, brown spots, and saggy skin. So, we just have to work a bit harder to get past the things that bother us. We can ignore them or combine our own DIY rituals with a little medical intervention, now that we know the latter is actually not scary or phony . . . just expensive. The great part is it takes no or minimal downtime to get us back out there ASAP and who's to know whether we're having a laser treatment? Even non-ablative lasers, ultrasound therapy, and radio frequency waves are losing their sci-fi strangeness. We do have choices. Nothing lasts forever—not even cosmetic surgery but it can free you for a while to concentrate on other things.

CHANGING UP OUR LOOKS.

It's not so much maintaining the way we used to look our best, but finding *a new best*. This is the time when we make big U-turns. We go from blonde to gray or vice versa, chop off our hair or at least chop in layers and bangs, finally go to a nutritionist to find out if we have food allergies or a food addiction, switch from wearing mostly black to wearing more color, leave our heels in the past and march forward in flats, or get our feet fixed and find pumps that don't kill our tootsies.

FINDING A NEW BALANCE AND RHYTHM TO OUR LIVES.

Here's the truth. We're not disconnecting from work so easily. We like earning money and value our work. We're taking more "staycations" and cruises that eliminate the stress and planning of complicated itineraries. And when we do travel for work, adventure, and once-in-a-lifetime trips, we've learned the smart moves pros use (see Chapter 2!). We're not novices. We all need downtime to balance work and keep our relationships going at a good clip.

Q: Should I forget "aging gracefully" and just go for it?

A: That phrase has a new definition—
a little tinkering can de-stress and improve quality of life.
Now that's aging gracefully!

....

Every woman gets to 50 with a pre-fabricated idea of what the rest of her life will *probably* be like. Some of us who envisioned a quieter existence have had their program interrupted by financial upheavals, divorce, health issues, and family disruptions. The fairy tale of age and retirement is gone and the curtain has been pulled back to reveal the behind-the-scenes grit and guts part. This is where that strength of character and backbone we've spent decades building come in handy.

....

BEEN THERE, DONE THAT

Every birthday I make a new to-do list. Some things dribble down year to year and never actually get done but go back on that list. These include reclaiming my original ambition as an illustrator and painter, going back to my fashion design roots—maybe creating a line of chic, light head-to-toe swimsuits with UPF-50+ for women 50+, teaching a class in print and online fashion journalism at my old training ground, Parsons School of Design, and learning something new—a language, maybe, or a craft. The list is a reminder to say *stay fluid*—open to new ideas, solutions, and opportunities. I channel anxiety as an energizer and excitement generator. I never think about what could go wrong, only what could go right. There are some things I longed to do or do again that I now know will never happen . . . so they're not on the list anymore. I'm a realist. At one time I dreamed of living in a thatched cottage in England with my horse, pack of dogs, and a wild garden, becoming an art restoration expert for a major museum, going back to school, and becoming a plastic surgeon. Now my list is focused on what I can accomplish, what I need to do, what I'd like to do, in more down-to-earth pragmatic terms. Onward!

LOIS'S TUTORIAL OF TRICKS #8

WE GET IT! 10 THINGS YOU'RE FINALLY READY FOR

Think of this list as the stuff you really couldn't handle until your fully formed B-Babe self got a grip on life. Some are not-so-quick fixes that take courage but will make you healthier and keep you that way, others are indulgences to pull you out of a rut, give you a break, or push you into a new way of thinking about age, your looks, and your life. It's finally time to:

1 FIX YOUR HIGH-HEEL LOVING FEET.

When Kathie Lee Gifford told me about her life-changing "bunionectomies" at an AARP lunch in NYC, the sparkling B-babe said her ability to zip around on 3- and 4-inch Manolos is due to the surgery. Women have a love/hate relationship with high heels. We love the way they make our legs look, love sitting in them, hate walking in them. Big problem. Bunions are huge lumps that protrude on the sides of your feet at the base of the big toes. Often accompanied by hammertoes, a condition where the second, third, or pinkie toes curl under like claws, both are the result of being squeezed into high heels with tight pointy toes. Our feet are complicated and each foot has 26 bones, 33 joints, and 126 muscles, ligaments, and nerves.

Bunion surgery means the removal and/or realignment of bone and tissue and a recovery period of 6 weeks to several months, stitches, pins, a walking cast, and possibly special shoes for a while but . . . it is a cure!

While Kathie Lee is a trouper, I'd opt for lower heels post-surgery (and even Manolos come in 1- and 2-inch heels!) so the pressure on the ball of the foot and toe box is decreased!

2 GO CRUISING!

Those Viking River Cruise commercials on PBS are hypnotic as we envision ourselves floating down French canals in luxury with none of the usual vacation hassles. No planning, no worries about over-packing, no hotels, or language difficulties. You're in a dreamy, contained situation with someone else taking care of the details. Of course, we could also sail the Caribbean in peace with a private balcony or float through Southeast Asia with 5,000 other people 50+, but rivers have no waves so no seasickness!

B-Babes are loving river cruises for their sophistication, refinement, and ability to travel intimately through cities like Amsterdam, Paris, Vienna, and Budapest in a personal but cultural way.

Ocean-going cruises vary a lot in looks, taste, and pricing so do your homework online and check peer reviews. There are destination-themed trips that attract our crowd—like food and wine; mind, body, and spirit; golf; film and theater; jazz with concerts; and panel discussions, lectures, and performances for brainiacs, culture, and sports enthusiasts. On sea cruises, grab a midship cabin above sea level (but not too high) with a balcony for fresh air and start taking over-the-counter motion sickness meds two days prior to sailing. Pack ginger tea, green apples, and crackers (trust me on this!).

AUDREY SMALTZ

What's on my bucket list? Gayle and I would love to go to China and see more of Africa. I'd like to take a course at the Art Students League and work in watercolors. I'd like to really learn how to speak French for conversation, not just my little hello-goodbye-restaurant phrases. For my 80th birthday I'd love to throw a fabulous party in Vegas.

3 CUT YOUR HAIR SHORT FOR THE FIRST TIME.

Robin Wright's short hair has started a trend. Yeah, Judy Dench, Halle Berry, and Jamie Lee Curtis beat her in the snip race but their cuts have a gamine or boyish quality; Wright's has sex appeal as does Kris Jenner's shortie. Is it a good idea for you? If you've been wearing your hair pulled back in a ponytail every day, you're ready.

➤ **There are short, shorter, and shortest options.** If you've had long hair forever, make a chin-length bob with texture or longer layers your try-out before going shorter.

➤ **Go short but add long, heavy bangs.** It feels like more hair, hides crow's feet and forehead lines, and is eye-peeking flirtatious.

➤ **A modified "fro" left natural and curly** is a statement and deserves the kick of bold hair color, statement glasses, earrings, or a lipstick for punctuation.

➤ **Look at your body, neck, jaw, and shape.** It's not just about the hair. Short hair works for women with athletic or curvy firm bodies, those with a well-shaped head and good profile, and B-babes with enormous style and charisma of any shape and size.

4 GET MOHS SURGERY ALREADY.

Okay, you put if off and put it off, finally had a biopsy, and you have to get that basal or squamous cell carcinoma off your nose! Don't worry, it's all done under local anesthetic so you won't feel anything. Here's how it goes. Dr. Robert Anolik of the Laser & Skin Surgery Center of New York says, "Mohs surgery is still the most effective method of removal for skin cancers from cosmetically and functionally significant sites like the face. Layers of skin containing the cancer are progressively cut away within very narrow margins to keep as much healthy skin intact as possible. Each removed layer is processed and examined under a microscope at the time of surgery." So you sit, fingers crossed, in the waiting room. If any remaining tumor is identified, you're outta luck, babe. A return for another pass is necessary. "The wound is then extended for further examination, and the process is repeated until the area is cancer-free. Mohs surgeons often close the wound with stitches but sometimes a skin graft (usually taken from the ear area) is necessary to repair the skin seamlessly." Clear your schedule for the day and bring a book.

5 MOTHERHOOD.

Becoming a mom for the first time at 50+ is a mini trend as more mature women decide to have or adopt a child late in life. We're living longer, have the finances, and emotional stability to enjoy a new addition to our lives without the pressures of our younger years. Some women in their 50s put off having kids and made work a priority, others never married or divorced and focused their energies elsewhere, and now older single women craving kids realize they have enough money, energy, and are in good health to do so even in their sixth decade. Adoption of a baby or child under 12 is always a possibility though with surrogate moms, biological freezing of eggs, IVF, and sperm donors,. It's even possible to have your own child after menopause! Getting the right level of advice, care, and support is essential.

6 FIND OUT WHETHER GOLD OR SILVER LOOK BETTER ON YOU.

Of course, you can combine all your metals—anything goes. But one metal is really going to make you glow more than the other. Do a mirror test wearing no makeup and overload the accessories to really get the idea. First pile on lots of gold pieces (earrings, necklaces, bracelets, rings), and then do another test with all silvery ones. Get ready. One group will emphasize dingy teeth, brown spots, and wrinkles and do nothing to enhance your hair color or skin while the other will soften lines and discolorations and make your hair color and complexion luminous. You don't have to give either up, just good to know going forward. It'll also help in choosing metal eyeglass frames and watches. In general:

➤ **Cool-toned silvery metals like silver, titanium, white gold, platinum, rose quartz, blue turquoise, amethyst, and pearls** flatter hair that's silver, white, a salt-and-pepper mix, or ashy brown; skin with cool pinky or blue undertones from palest ivory to deepest ebony; and blue, violet, gray, or very dark eyes.

➤ **Gold and warm gems like jade, peridot, citrine, coral, amber, carnelian, tiger's eye yellow, and green turquoise** usually flatter blondes, redheads, and brunettes with golden highlights; skin with warm, golden, peachy, terra-cotta undertones; eyes with golden glints—like hazel, green, or brown.

7 FIND YOUR IDEAL FOUNDATION EVERY YEAR.

The texture, shade, and possibly even the brand you choose will change and update every 12 months. Improvements and innovation in makeup are getting more refined. Don't get caught up by trends, specific categories like BB, CC, DD and words like naked, camera-ready, invisible, or HD on the label . . . although one of these may well be your ultimate solution. Your goal is to find a liquid, serum, or cream makeup that fits like a second skin no matter what it's called.

If you're an online beauty shopper, know your MAC makeup shade. Consumers who do product reviews and ratings often refer to their prescribed MAC shade—like W120 or NC40 or NW35, for example—as a universal guideline for determining shades for any brand. Eyeballing shades is tough on a screen, though L'Oréal Paris (lorealparisusa.com) has online interactive tools to help find your best formula and shade matches and Bobbi Brown (bobbibrowncosmetics.com) offers "talk to an artist" shade and texture advice and you can upload a photo for an online consultation. Sephora.com gives very detailed shade descriptions for most brands and Sephora stores have the Color IQ service. This is a handheld scanning device that matches your complexion to an edited list of perfect options from 1,500 formulas. No store nearby? You can get new foundation suggestions color matched online at Sephora.com even if you don't have a Color IQ number yet by inputting the foundation and shade you usually wear. Take advantage of these and stop wasting time and money on duds!

CAROL E. CAMPBELL

I think I'm a happier person and more well rounded than I used to be. I'm a better friend and I'm finally ready for a true intimate relationship with a partner. All the stuff that happened in my 20s, 30s, and 40s was prep work!

8 IDEAL BASICS.

No more fooling around. You're a grown-up and 90 percent of the "basics" out there are too trendy, poorly made, or lacking in substance and style to make them worthy of us. You're going to be wearing these items at least 100 times this year, so splurge. Only a handful of resources have exactly what we want.

➤ **Your perfect T-shirt** has a neckline that's not too prim or low and comes in a fabric that's not too sheer or stiff. Buy cotton jersey, viscose, or a cotton/modal blend so it *feels* soft and thin but in reality is opaque enough to not show your bra. The neckline should be a scoop, boat, or V since they layer easily over and under other pieces. A longer, relaxed length of 25 or 26 inches to adequately cover all, a drop-tail curved hem slightly longer in back, or side slits for a half-tucked friendly shape with short clean and classic three-quarter or long sleeves are exactly right. And once you find it stock up in your favorite neutrals—gray, white, navy, and black. Good places to look: Madewell, J. Crew, Eileen Fisher, Splendid, Rag & Bone, and Everlane.

➤ **Your everyday pullover sweater** should have a shallow scoop or a V neck, a longer and slightly relaxed fit at the hem but high armholes in light knits like merino wool, cashmere, and cotton/viscose blends. Good places to look: Madewell and J. Crew.

➤ **Your basic tailored blazer** now is navy (looks great with black and jeans) in a stretch blend cotton or wool with a slim single-breasted shape and a notch collar. Though everyone from Gucci to Yves Saint Laurent makes them, your best bets are: Theory, J. Crew, Rag & Bone, and Club Monaco.

➤ **Your ankle cropped pants** (sometimes found in the capri category online) will be a tailored stretch blend like cotton/rayon/spandex, stretch wool, or a soft and slouchy version in a viscose jersey. All should sit at your natural waist, have slim or straight legs, and look equally great with flats or heels. Good places to find: J. Crew, Theory, Everlane, and Eileen Fisher.

9 USING APPS TO SHOP SMARTER AND FASTER.

No smart online shopper wants to pay more than she has to for a pair of amazing shoes, a quality bag for work, a dress, or an entire outfit she covets. No point spending your time looking for the best buy, either. Let AppCrawlr, an app search engine, help you finds the best apps and online shopping sites with flash sales like HauteLook, NordstromRack, Ideel, and MyHabit, which are all free. RedLaser (an app) scans the barcode of an item you're after and compares competitor prices and reviews. ShopStyle is a search engine that instantly filters the web for whatever you need at a price you can afford. Stylr shows you what's on sale in your neighborhood and the Hunt is like a personal shopper—you post a picture of what you're looking for and it tells you where to find it cheap. Neat! Also know the websites that edit and filter the items we look for most often. Try: Net-a-Porter, Shopbop, J. Crew, La Garçonne, Sephora, 1010 Park Place (my chum Brenda Coffee's site for women 50+—see her in this book!), Mango, and Zara for can't miss solutions.

10 HAVE A REAL EDGE.

A hint of darkness in our character at 50 is subtle, not something that can be faked with a few skull rings. Edge gives us an edge . . . in work, relationships, and life. It can come across in a sexy lower-pitched voice that purrs or the ability to wear shape-hugging clothing that only hints in a provocative way—a cold-shoulder black cashmere sweater, a conservative high-neck LBD with a low V back, smoldering kohl-rimmed eyes (I loved legendary Italian journalist Oriana Fallaci's black-lined gaze). We're sensual and never coy. We don't display our boobs, get sloppy-drunk, or dance on tables, but we exude an irresistible force that makes us magnetic.

SASS TALK: WHAT EXACTLY ARE YOU WAITING FOR?!

So much pressure to do things from here to eternity—all pushed by the media and friends who always are first to do whatever's hot. You've never been to Prague or Panama? Never eaten Thai food in Thailand or swum with dolphins? Never had fillers? So much to do, so much time to do it since we're living longer, healthier lives.

ALISON HOUTTE

I'm an intense tennis player—a 4.0, which means I'm good! I want to move to south Florida and play on 4 different tennis leagues, eat avocados right off the tree, and be in greener surroundings. I'll be wearing boatloads of sunblock, but no cosmetic surgery for me! I'd love to have a vintage boutique truck on wheels—like a gourmet food truck but for fashion.

JUST BETWEEN US:
10 THINGS EVERY GUTSY WOMAN CONSIDERS

"Okay, what on earth did she do to her face?" "Is that her real hair?" "She must have had lap band surgery—she's not been that thin in 20 years." That's the chatter we never want to hear about ourselves. Recently I've been catching up with chums (everyday, no-celeb women 50+) I haven't seen in a while. Some have "new" taut faces, over-inflated, lips and Joker-like grins stretching ear to ear. Others have clearly gotten their boobs done, a tummy tuck, or enough filler to inflate the Macy's Thanksgiving Day Parade floats. Girls, I'm all for "freshening up," but you've got to know when enough is enough!

According to the American Society for Aesthetic Plastic Surgery, we spent more than $11 billion on surgical and non-surgical procedures in 2014. NYC face and reconstructive plastic surgeon Dr. Konstantin Vasyukevich says, "I think if a facelift and other procedures are done well, no one should be able to tell you've had them. The goal is to make you look more youthful, not different." When friends ask why you look so good, saying "great skincare and a healthy lifestyle" isn't far from the truth. Here's how to take up the slack, fix the stuff that bothers you, and still look like you. You just may want to spring for:

1 A HAIR TRANSPLANT.

Try Minoxidil first, the OTC drug sold in drugstores as Rogaine for thinning hair. For serious hair-loss issues, see a dermatologist who specializes in hair loss to determine the cause and extent. For women with female pattern hair baldness and seriously sparse hairlines, a hair transplant operation is worth the $15,000, or so I'm told. A good chum had one and was willing to dish anonymously. Three years after the procedure she doesn't have the hair she had at 35, but she has a full head of hair where she had truly skimpy, balding locks before. You do need to have enough hair in back at the nape to supply plugs and work as a donor area. The procedure is long—a full day—and done in-office, but you're given numbing Lidocaine injections at the scalp and are on IV sedation and don't feel a thing. The hair that's to be removed from the donor area or "harvested "is taken away in strips. Then a team gets busy dividing the strips into teeny units of 2 to 4 hairs at a time that get re-implanted and stitched in place where needed. There's numbness afterward but no pain, no dressings, and the stitches are removed a week later. Between 6 and 8 months later you see new regrowth.

2 PERMANENT MAKEUP.

Permanent makeup is a micropigment form of facial tattooing and trending up for women 50+. Yes, waking up every day with perfectly formed full brows, defined eyes, and shapely lips tinted a youthful pinky-tan sounds appealing, but few technicians are masters of this art. The good news is that brow, eye, and lip tattoos are being offered as procedures at more top dermatological and cosmetic surgery practices so ask your doctor for referrals.

Cosmetic tattoos can replicate full brows, crisp up aging eyes with 24/7 liner, and restore shape to flattened lips that have lost volume plus a baby fresh rosy hue. According to dermatologist Dr. Doris Day, "this requires skill and an eye for color to get a natural enhanced look. Permanent black eyeliner can fade over time, turning a blue-gray shade so be aware you may need retouching." You'll need a patch test first to rule out sensitivity and time away from Retin-A, Botox, fillers, contacts, and artificial tears (if you opt for eyeliner). During healing you can't swim, take hot steamy showers, baths, or saunas, and if you're prone to cold sores, no lip tattoos for you! Dyes take weeks to settle into their real color and will look much darker at first, so don't be scared!

3 A SCALPEL-FREE FACE-LIFT.

You should *not* look like you have golf balls in your cheeks!

No cutting! What are you waiting for? Botox and fillers—2 minimally invasive procedures are up according to a 2015 report from the American Society of Plastic Surgeons. Be sure to choose a board-certified cosmetic dermatologist with extensive experience. Dermatologist Dr. Jeanette Graf says, "If you're a good candidate for filler, start with the midface—that's where women usually need the most help. You want to inject filler at the apex of the cheekbone for definition. This will lift up saggy, jowly skin of the lower face without using filler in the nasolabial fold. Filling the outside of the face at the cheekbone gives you a sculpted look—you should *not* look like you have golf balls in your cheeks! Filler in the lower face only creates a heavy triangular look to your face."

The new filler Belotero works for fine lines around the lips and crow's feet. According to NYC dermatologist Dr. Debra Jaliman, "There may be bruising, so do fillers 2 weeks before a big event. If you want volume at the cheeks for a youthful look, your best bet now is Voluma—but best done gradually (1 syringe per visit, wait a week, and then do another syringe or 2). Other fillers—Restylane, Perlane, or Juvederm also work to fill the cheeks so the nasolabial fold, and 'marionette lines'—the grooves from corners of your mouth to chin—are smoothed."

According to NYC cosmetic surgeon Dr. Konstantin Vasyukevich, "Filler lasts for about 1 to 2 years, but avoid frequent repeats. It makes women's faces look overfilled and distorted."

4 AN EYE JOB.

Blepharoplasty is surgery that repairs droopy upper lids and/or bags under your eyes by removing excess skin, muscle, and fat. It instantly removes a "tired" look. Recovery is fast—a long 4-day weekend and pastel-tinted eyeglass lenses hide swelling and bruises until all heals. In some cases, an eye lift can improve peripheral vision by removing excess skin that's blocking your vision and may be covered by Medicare. Don't go for an extreme pull or lift at the outer eye. Top NYC plastic surgeon Dr. Barry Weintraub says, "If you take too much skin and fat from the upper lids the patient has that dreaded deer-in-the-headlights look, making them look done and older. A good surgeon will preserve the original attractive shape of your youthful eyes." One week later, you're back in business and dabbling with your makeup again.

Dermatologist Dr. Debra Jaliman cautions, "Never do your eyes twice. If you've had a scalpel eye lift in your 30s or 40s to correct sag or bags, a liquid lift is all you need now. Botox injected along the brows lifts droopy tails and relaxes crow's feet since the same muscle controls both. Filler injected in the tear trough groove lifts and lightens so your eyes look bigger."

5 CLEANED-UP CLEAVAGE.

Why keep hiding out in turtlenecks when a V neckline emphasizes our shoulders, whittles our waist, and provides a pretty amazing neck-stretching focal point? The reason is what top dermatologists now call "dirty chest." That's what a décolletage covered with brown spots, broken capillaries, and uneven "chicken skin" looks like. Top NYC dermatologist Gervaise Gerstner says "neck and chest therapy are a priority for women in their 50s now. They may have been diligent about high SPF sunscreen for the face but neglected the chest completely or relied on a low SPF for the body, during years of earlier sunbathing."

Dr. Debra Jaliman adds, "The IPL (Intense Pulsed Laser) is very effective and can be done multiple times, usually waiting a month between treatments, which can number anywhere from 1 to 3 sessions. Also the Fraxel re:store Dual laser is very good for a sun-damaged cleavage, too." And that everyday plain cotton T-shirt has only about an SPF 10 and sun goes right through it. You need to wear a high SPF 30+ sunscreen under your usual tee or one with built-in Ultraviolet Protection Factor (UVF) that give consistent protection. A whole new category of what's called rash-guard tees and sun-protected clothing has anywhere from UVF 15 to 50 depending on the brand. J. Crew, Coolibar, Parasol, Patagonia, and Mott 50 all have them.

6 AN EAR MAKEOVER.

The combo of hearing aids, long floppy ear lobes (that keep growing with age) and stretched-out piercings is a bad one. Too much going on in a small area. Get your ears to a cosmetic dermatologist or plastic surgeon and have stretched-out or even torn piercings repaired. It's not a complicated procedure but allow 6 to 8 weeks for healing before repiercing. And for droopy earrings, a shot of filler such as Restylane or Juvederm will plump up thin lobes—so your dazzling 5-carat studs won't flop.

7 SAYING BUH-BYE TO BROWN SPOTS.

Block out a 4-day weekend to clean up the crud for good with the new Fraxel re:store Dual laser. Dr. Robert Anolik of the Laser & Skin Surgery Center of New York, says "Expect redness like bad sunburn on day 2, then bronzing of the skin and extreme peeling. But a gentle sonic skin brush on a low setting can speed exfoliation and get you back in the game fast." Also know that the "downtime" of laser recovery gets longer as you go down the body. Dr. Anolik adds, "If a laser is strong enough to blast and heal facial brown spots in 3 days, it may take 10 days to 2 weeks on the forearm, chest, or hands."

BRENDA COFFEE

Because I'm not afraid of the word "no" I ask for what I want. As a result, I've led an adventurous life and have already done most of my bucket list things, like fly an Air Force fighter jet and land on an Air Force carrier, and I've been at deep ocean depths in a nuclear submarine. From here, I want to have my own online talk show and rent an apartment in Paris or a villa in Italy and spend at least a month living there. And I'd love for Patti Hansen and Keith Richards to take me shopping for a 50+ rocker chic look!

8 REDOING YOUR HANDS.

Dark and trendy nail polish shades have given every woman 50+ who wants "edge" exactly that. The problem is, the more attention we call to our hands, we also focus on the saggy, crepey, spotty, veiny skin. Hands lose fat and collagen just like our faces and deflate. According to Dr. Joshua Zeichner, "Fillers like Radiesse, Juvederm, or Perlane injected carefully can lift the skin slightly for a more cushioned, youthful look, while lasers can erase brown spots."

9 A BREAST LIFT OR REDUCTION.

Droopy big boobs don't get any easier to dress even if the rest of your body is toned and trim. NYC cosmetic and reconstructive surgeon Dr. Kenneth R. Francis says, "Many 50-year-old women are now in better shape than when they were 20. I suggest working with your body proportions, though a reduction to a C cup is average and fits most body types." Reductions are satisfying operations. If you've been carrying around two 3- to 4-pound weights for 35 years (allowing for breasts to reach full size in your midteens), the benefits to neck and back discomfort and agility are phenomenal.

"A breast lift is slightly different. Usually one of the things contributing to sagging is loss of volume and subsequent loosening of the skin. For this reason, it's often necessary to restore volume with small implants or even fat transfer when performing a breast lift in patients over 50. For women who don't want volume added, a lift alone can be performed, of course." Dr. Francis says both reductions and lifts are relatively pain-free with a supportive bra required around the clock for 6 weeks to allow scars to strengthen. "Light exercise can usually be resumed within 2 to 3 weeks."

10 GET YOUR NOSE LIFTED.

Noses, like ears, continue to grow as we age, so even those who have not had rhinoplasty are considering a tip plasty now. Women who had nose jobs in their youth often experience tip issues after 50—too droopy, bulbous, or downturned when smiling. NYC facial plastic and reconstructive surgeon Dr. Konstantin Vasyukevich says, "Tip plasty, if done correctly, gives a natural look so you won't see a radically different face, just an improved profile and expression when you smile."

Noses—authentic or enhanced earlier in life—continue to grow longer as we age. One solution is to reposition the tip upward as a mini noselift. This does not change your nose, just improves it. "Bad old nose jobs can be difficult to fix since surgery back in the day significantly changed the internal support, which over time resulted in buckling of the cartilage and other irregularities at the tip. In cases like this, a whole new rhinoplasty has to be done—with the nose rebuilt by skilled work."

BROADMINDED: HOW YOUTHFUL DO YOU NEED TO LOOK?

Beauty is in the mind of the beholder. Each of the 11 women profiled in this book was asked the above question. All emphasized they want to look "as great as possible" but none wanted to look "young." In fact, a few laughed and said they look their best right now and never think about age at all. Each of us has her own idea of "looking good" at 50+. The inner/outer beauty thing we speak of so often works 2 different ways. For some women it's all about the confidence and self-assurance within. Then they can blow off saggy lids and tired eyes with makeup, slip out of bloat mode and into whatever looks good that day, add their sexy shoes, statement glasses, and take off feeling like a million. For others it works the other way around. When their hair is freshly fixed, their nails just done, Botox finally kicking in, and they're wearing a look-at-me dress, the inner motor gets turbo-charged with self-assurance, inspiration, and *then* they're unstoppable, unbeatable, and unforgettable. Everyone thinks about cosmetic surgery and dermatological procedures . . . even if they haven't done them.

Top NYC cosmetic surgeon to the rich and famous Dr. David Rosenberg says, "It's a scary vision for patients and doctors to see aesthetics gone awry. It creates a fear factor. Bad face-lifts are not accidents—the surgeon's judgment is off." To practice medicine in the U.S. all you need to be is a licensed doctor. Board-certified doctors go beyond basic licensing to meet higher standards to practice in a specialty field. You don't want your internist or dentist doing Botox or facial filler. Any dermatologist or cosmetic surgeon you select must be board-certified. This means he or she must be qualified to practice in that specific medical field and meet standards that go way beyond basics. Each doctor has to keep up with the latest advances in their specialty—so that in terms of procedures, equipment, and patients safety, you get the best care. The following websites can help you locate board-certified cosmetic and reconstructive surgeons in your area:

➤ **The American Academy of Cosmetic Surgery** (AACS) at cosmeticsurgery.org

➤ **The American Society of Plastic Surgeons** at www.plasticsurgeons.org

> **The American Board of Cosmetic Surgery** at americanboardcosmeticsurgery.org

> **The American Society for Aesthetic Plastic Surgery** (ASAPS) at surgery.org

> **The American Academy of Dermatology** (AAD) at aad.org.

And when you do book a consultation, ask to see examples of before and after work done by the doctor of the procedure you have in mind and how many he's performed. Most women have friends who've had work done and are eager to share their doctor's name and number. But . . . there's good work and bad. Here's how to tell the difference with advice from Dr. Konstantin Vasyukevich:

> **Frozen Face:** When Botox is overdone, the face lacks the ability to express emotion and the brows may be overly elevated. Both of these problems are easy to fix—a little less Botox in the first case and a touch more in the second would make the face appear more natural. Good Botox relaxes facial muscles for at least 3 to 4 months but there is a window when you begin to see muscle activity returning when you see wrinkles. Hold off and avoid repeats too soon.

> **Chipmunk cheeks:** Too much filler has been used to add volume. The smile gives it all away since smiling already elevates and enhances the contours of the upper face; too much fullness in the form of overly puffy, high cheeks indicates a mistake.

> **Triangle face:** A bottom-heavy lower face is not a "fix." Nasolabial folds and marionette lines that are filled lead to a wide, heavy-looking lower face, especially when added to jowls that continue to sag with age.

> **Cat eyes:** A dramatic change in the shape of the eyes with excessive pulling is the result of too much cutting—often less is more here. Sometimes the bottom lids droop too much as well when lower lids are incorrectly done.

> **Pulled-back face:** An overly taut face with ears and hairline stretched and distorted is seen less in new face-lifts than old ones. Advanced surgical techniques give a natural look.

Looking ahead, my personal bucket list is endless. I want to shake off any residual age hang-ups that may still be lurking in my mind. Recently I grew out my bangs—anticipating frizz-free travel to tropical climates and more swimming on the agenda. This was a biggie because bangs make me look more youthful, have been my peek-a-boo answer to Botox for 15 years, and my husband thinks I look "cuter" with them. All true! They're *baaack*. I've been wearing more eye makeup 24/7 than ever before—heavy on the kohl and brown shadow, and a chignon or big messy Bardot-y 'do, going for an aging Bolshoi ballerina/rock-star look. I've started a witty, crazy 50+ comic strip using my friends, family, and work colleagues as the basis for the cartoon characters and content because the things they say and do at this point make me laugh and are better than anything on *Girls*. And if enough of you buy this book and write 5-star-reviews online, we can keep this conversation going till we're 100! Let's talk sooner rather than later!

xxoo Lois

THANK YOU FROM LOIS!

Despite my reputation as a sassy know-it-all, *The Woman's Wakeup* has truly been a collaboration. My gutsy gang of 11 women superstars, my charismatic photo crew, my crack hair and makeup team, my Running Press posse, and my A-list medical advisors and beauty pros all were there beside me and know the truth ... that women 50+ rule the world!

Let's not mince words here. My chums and buds:

Alison Houtte: Vintage magician who can pull an Hermès bag out of thin air.

Audrey Smaltz: Fashionable firecracker who makes runways and charity galas sizzle.

Brenda Coffee: Adventurer and reinventor who lives at 1010 Park Place.

Carol E. Campbell: aka The Moneymaker, who leverages dating to new levels.

Donna Bunte: Healthy-eating ambassador and holistic healer on a mission.

Jeannine Shao Collins: Publisher who always wants and gets *MORE* from life.

Karen Oliver: Beauty curator, couturier, and PR pro with a twist.

Maury Rogoff: Bi-coastal PR diva with wit and shopping skills a stylist would envy.

Myrna Blyth: Publishing-industry legend and my lifelong mentor.

Nancy Ganz Steir: Revolutionary thinker who started the modern shapewear industry.

Rene Syler: A "Good Enough Mother" and a star on any set she steps foot.

Michael Waring: My super-talented photographer who shot the entire book with the flu in the middle of winter (like a combo of Daniel Craig and Johnny Depp only with a camera).

Fiona Breslin: My spirited assistant who will be a fashion power broker someday.

Alexander "Woodchuck" Yerks: For spot-on photo tech and conjuring tricks.

Joe "Coffee" Leonard: For his flirtability on set and patience.

Christian Torres: For backup charm.

Carmel Bianco: Of the Ray Brown Pro Agency, for hair wizardry, volume, and my new favorite hair clips from Ricky's!

Janeiro Gonzales: Of Art Department Agency, for Oscar-worthy lashes and lipstick.

Everyone at Shoot Digital: My home away from home . . . but especially Hector.

Cindy De La Hoz: My editor, champion, and wordsmith genie for pushing this book into being and making it even better.

Frances Soo Ping Chow: My creative director for making the book come alive visually and understanding my passion to get it right.

Alice Martell: My lifelong agent, confidante, and friend for life who fights my battles.

Dr. Debra Jaliman: A dermatologist with a clientele of top models, editors, and media stars who knows her way around a syringe.

Dr. Doris Day: A dermatologist with a celeb-packed NYC practice and MelaFind!

Dr. Jeanette Graf: A cutting-edge NYC dermatologist with wit and a love of peptides.

Dr. Gervaise Gerstner: A Park Avenue dermatologist who banishes brown spots.

Dr. Joshua Zeichner: Director of Cosmetic and Clinical Research in Dermatology at Mount Sinai Hospital.

Dr. Robert Anolik: Of the Laser & Skin Surgery Center of New York and laser guru.

Dr. Robert Dorin: NYC hair specialist and restoration surgeon.

Dr. Marc Lowenberg: Cosmetic dentist of Lowenberg, Lituchy & Kantor in NYC.

Dr. Konstantin Vasyukevich: NYC facial plastic and reconstructive surgeon extraordinaire.

Dr. Kenneth R. Francis: NYC cosmetic and reconstructive surgeon who knows breasts!

Dr. Paul Jarrod Frank: Founder and director of the 5th Avenue Dermatology Surgery and Laser Center.

Dr. David Rosenberg: NYC cosmetic surgeon to the rich and famous.

Chris Cusano: Style maker at the Brad Johns Color Studio at the Samuel Shriqui Salon in NYC.

Julius Michael: Star colorist and co-owner of the Julius Michael Salon in Scarsdale, New York.

Brad Johns: Master colorist at the Brad Johns Color Studio at the Samuel Shriqui Salon in NYC.

My daughters Jennifer Jolie and Alexandra Jade, who are my 24/7 cheerleaders.

My husband Robert R. Kadanoff (aka "Sweetie"), who spent an icy cold winter in New York instead of playing golf somewhere sunny and warm so I could write this book!

INDEX